Aging N

Aging Matters

*Finding Your Calling
for the Rest of Your Life*

R. Paul Stevens

William B. Eerdmans Publishing Company
Grand Rapids, Michigan / Cambridge, U.K.

Published 2016 by

Wm. B. Eerdmans Publishing Co.

2140 Oak Industrial Drive N.E., Grand Rapids, Michigan 49505 /

P.O. Box 163, Cambridge CB3 9PU U.K.

www.eerdmans.com

Printed in the United States of America

22 21 20 19 18 17 16   7 6 5 4 3 2 1

Library of Congress Cataloging-in-Publication Data

Names: Stevens, R. Paul, 1937-   author.

Title: Aging matters : finding your calling for the rest of your life / R.   Paul Stevens.

Description: Grand Rapids, Michigan : Eerdmans Publishing Company, 2016. |

Includes bibliographical references and index.

Identifiers: LCCN 2015045472 | ISBN 9780802872333 (pbk. : alk. paper)

Subjects: LCSH: Older Christians — Religious life.

Classification: LCC BV4580 .S702 2016 | DDC 248.8/5 — dc23

LC record available at http://lccn.loc.gov/2015045472

Contents

Contents

Introduction

Success in retirement depends in great measure on the way we lived beforehand.

Paul Tournier[1]

Old age was not a defeat but a victory, not a punishment but a privilege.

Abraham Heschel[2]

At seventy-eight years of age I am not quite in the "oldest-olds" category but certainly on the way. According to recent studies even old age now is sub-categorized. Young-olds are sixty to sixty-nine; old-olds are seventy to seventy-nine; and oldest-olds are eighty-plus.[3] So I have a vested interest in writing this book, not only for myself but for many friends who also are facing their senior years, many of them with more physical ailments than I. How are we to

1. Paul Tournier, *Learn to Grow Old*, trans. Edwin Hudson (Louisville, KY: Westminster John Knox Press, 1972), p. 19.
2. Abraham J. Heschel, *The Insecurity of Freedom* (New York: Schocken Books, 1972), 71-72, quoted in James M. Houston and Michael Parker, *A Vision for the Aging Church: Renewing Ministry for and by Seniors* (Downers Grove, IL: IVP Academic, 2011), p. 55.
3. George Vaillant, *Aging Well* (New York: Little, Brown, 2002), p. 23.

think of these years? More importantly, how are we to live? And how are we to live with faith (no matter your faith tradition)? Does our calling, that delightful summons on our life that gives meaning and purpose, end with formal retirement? (I retired eight years ago.) Should retirement be redefined, "reframed" as they say today, which means looking at it from an entirely different perspective, through a different lens? Walter Wright in *The Third Third of Life* observes, "Retirement is being redefined."[4]

Here is another question: Does aging increase our spirituality, that heart for transcendence, or soul search? Are there special vices and virtues in aging, and spiritual disciplines to enable us to grow spiritually in our most senior years? What is our legacy? What are we leaving behind? And how are we to think about and live towards death, as there is a one hundred percent certainty that we will die? Nobody fails this one. But that raises the question of the next life and whether it would be a good thing to prolong our life indefinitely on earth. These are the haunting questions we will take up in this book.

Frankly, I am writing for myself, but also for you, my reader, who may also be caring for aging parents. If you are a social worker or care giver, wanting to understand what aging means and how to go about it fruitfully, how to help others face it and thrive through it, this is for you. Since this book is about aging it is, truly, about everyone. I will be approaching these questions from the perspective of a Christian faith, and I will be drawing on the Scriptures of the Jewish and Christian people groups. There are rich resources for people of other traditions or some resources from people who have no faith at all.[5] But I am writing, I trust, in a way that could be accessed by people who are not at this point Jewish or Christian believers and who belong to another faith tradition. But I do so believing that there is within the Christian faith much to turn aging into an adventure and a blessing rather than a tragic de-

---

4. Walter C. Wright, *The Third Third of Life: Preparing for Your Future* (Downers Grove, IL: InterVarsity Press, 2012), p. 33.

5. See Richard John Neuhaus, ed., *The Eternal Pity: Reflections on Dying* (Notre Dame: University of Notre Dame Press, 2000).

nouement. One of my favorite Jewish authors, Abraham Heschel, says, "Old age was not a defeat but a victory, not a punishment but a privilege."[6] Heschel continues, "One ought to enter old age the way one enters the senior years at a university, in exciting anticipation of consummation. . . . They are indeed formative years, rich in possibilities to unlearn the follies of a lifetime, to see through inbred self-deceptions, to deepen understanding and compassion, to widen the horizon of honesty, to refine the sense of fairness."[7] But there is a further reason for this book.

The Gray Tsunami

There is no question that we have a population bulge in the seniors group that, on the population charts, is like an awkwardly large animal going through the long neck of snake. In the late Middle Ages those who survived to twenty could on average live to around fifty. In 1992, 12 percent of the U.S. population — something over thirty million people — were over sixty-five. By the best estimate, 18 percent of us will be that old by 2020. By 2040 one out of four North Americans will be sixty-five or over. In 1776, a child born in the United States had an average life expectancy of thirty-five. By the middle of the twenty-first century, it is expected in some generous estimates that men will live to 86 and women to 92.[8] "According to the Institute of Medicine, starting in 2011, a baby boomer [born between 1946 and 1964] will turn sixty-five every twenty seconds [in the United States]."[9] Baby boomers have delayed growing up, delayed marriage, delayed childbearing, delayed saving for retirement, and almost certainly are delaying retirement, sometimes for financial reasons. So what some have called the "second half" of life, roughly when one turns fifty (how

6. Heschel, *The Insecurity of Freedom*, 71-72, quoted in Houston and Parker, *A Vision for the Aging Church*, p. 55.

7. Quoted in Zalman Schachter-Shalomi, *From Age-ing to Sage-ing* (New York: Grand Central Publishing, 1995), pp. 21-22.

8. Schachter-Shalomi, *From Age-ing to Sage-ing*, p. 4.

9. Houston and Parker, *A Vision for the Aging Church*, p. 35.

many people do you know who are one hundred?), there is now what Walter Wright and others call the "third third." The first third (one to thirty), he explains, "we spend in incubation, education, preparation, exploring identity and purpose, intimacy and relationships." But then, from thirty to sixty, we enter a second third "dominated by family and work; we define our core relationships and commit to a career path." But then, from age sixty to ninety, we "encounter the unexplored terrain of life after the working career."[10] Formerly this territory was a short trip, but now with better health and longevity it can be much longer, even twenty to thirty years. "The point of this third third . . . is this: As we enter the third third of life, our calling will find new texture, new form, new possibilities."[11] Walter Wright describes a grandmother who "retired" for the first time in 1960 and then had four more careers: teaching, volunteering in the hospital, creating a historical society, and working for the library.[12] These striking examples of mid-life and late-life fruitfulness do not ameliorate the double message seniors and aging people hear from society.

How People and Society View Aging

On the one hand classic liberal economists tell us that population control and a declining birth rate are important for a healthy economy. But now, with fewer working persons to support the elderly, there is a crisis looming. Even the government pension plans, which are really in-and-out bank accounts, are in serious trouble because fewer are contributing to them and more are taking money out. So today older persons are often viewed as frail, sick, disabled, powerless, sexless, passive, alone, unloved, unable to learn, and burdensome. "Americans have come to view aging not as a fated aspect of our individual and social existence, but as one of life's problems to be solved through willpower, aided by science, technology, and

10. Wright, *The Third Third of Life*, p. 9.
11. Wright, *The Third Third of Life*, p. 16.
12. Wright, *The Third Third of Life*, p. 19.

expertise."[13] People fear aging partly because they fear death. The logic is circular. It is mostly old people who die. So we fear getting old because we will die. So aging is a paradox. Everyone wants to live longer, but none of us wants to get old.

One thing that is apparent in considering ancient texts and cultural artifacts is this: old age and death, prior to what we call the "modern era," were not clearly correlated as they are for us. We put death as the logical conclusion of a long life but the ancients, and even the early Christians, as well as people in much of the majority world, did not expect necessarily to live until old age. In this vein Augustine said, "No one has died who was not going to die at some time, and the end of life reduces the longest life to the same conclusion as the shortest. . . . What does it matter by what kind of death life is brought to an end."[14] There are even some gender differences. "Women face aging sooner and more realistically because they go through menopause," notes Lewis Richmond.[15] As one doctor said, "When it comes to realizing they're aging, women drop off the cliff, so to speak, while men the same age either ignore the signs or notice them a lot more gradually."[16]

So in this book we will first of all approach the question of aging in terms of calling or vocation. We will consider reframing retirement as a positive experience. We will ask whether we are supposed to work until we die, and how we should work. We will consider how we discern our calling for the rest of our lives. In this context we will note the many narratives and teachings in the Hebrew and Greek Scriptures as they relate to aging.

In the second section we will consider spirituality. We will consider whether the aging process itself is a spiritual discipline,

13. Carol Bailey Stoneking, "Modernity: The Social Construction of Aging," in Stanley Haurerwas et al., *Growing Old in Christ* (Grand Rapids: Eerdmans, 2003), p. 69.

14. Augustine, *City of God*, 1.11, quoted in Rowan Greer, "Special Gift and Special Burden: Views of Old Age in the Early Church," in Stanley Hauerwas et al., *Growing Old in Christ* (Grand Rapids: Eerdmans, 2003), p. 23.

15. Lewis Richmond, *Aging as a Spiritual Practice: A Contemplative Guide to Growing Older and Wiser* (New York: Gotham Books, 2012), p. 175.

16. Richmond, *Aging as a Spiritual Practice*, p. 175.

a spiritual journey, but we will also ask what vices and virtues are uniquely associated with aging.

In the third section we will consider leaving a multifaceted legacy. We will consider how to prepare for death and what there is on the other side.

In all this I will be presenting aging as a time of potential fruitfulness. A Jewish rabbi points to some exceptional examples of generativity in old age:

> Giuseppe Verdi composed *Otello* at age seventy-three and *Falstaff* when he was approaching eighty. Thomas Mann wrote *Dr. Faustus* and *Confessions of Felix Krull, Confidence Man* after age seventy, while Picasso was producing masterpieces into his nineties. Architect Frank Lloyd Wright began his most creative work at age sixty-nine; philosopher Alfred North Whitehead published his most influential works after sixty-five; and the mind of the scientist-visionary Buckminster Fuller was teeming with creative innovation at age eighty.[17]

Few of us will be this creative. But all of us can approach aging with a positive attitude and seize the special opportunities which this new situation affords. And we will explore these.

What You Can Gain from This Book

- Perspective — seeing advancing years as a process of maturing that is laden with new opportunities, including the opportunity to reframe the experience of retirement.
- Hope — recognizing that faith enables us to see an ultimate future that is even better than the past.
- Guidance — in discovering a refined sense of life purpose and meaning that is our "calling," our vocation.
- Spiritual and personal growth — in helping us see that the very process of aging is a spiritual journey in which we can, through

17. Schachter-Shalomi, *From Age-ing to Sage-ing*, pp. 43-44.

6

addressing vices, nurturing virtues, and developing spiritual disciplines, become more whole persons, more connected with God, with others, and with the created order.

• Practical guidelines — for addressing issues of will-making, doing late-life review, and preparing for death and the afterlife.

Dr. Paul Pearce — with whom I teach the "Aging Matters" course at Regent College and Carey Theological College — and Dr. Yuk Shuen Wong have outlined the "Factors Contributing to Healthy Aging." They list them in an article published in *BC Psychologist*. First, there is the vocational factor — realigning priorities and commitments, while staying motivated and interested with a meaningful use of time. Second is the wellness factor — taking responsibility for personal wellness and health. Third is the social factor — relationships, friendships, and community connections that provide a feeling of personal security and wellness. Fourth, there is the resources factor — not only having assurance that one has financial stability in time of a changed lifestyle, but also the personal equity and resources that can be used to make a meaningful contribution to family and community. Finally, there is the spiritual factor — a kind of "second chance" at increasing spiritual depth as we explore life's mysteries and our relationship with the supreme transcendent Other.[18] In this book we will be explore all of these factors.

How to Use This Book for All It's Worth

Of course the book can be read by individuals, whether aged, aging, or interested in helping older people. There are many footnotes which point to other resources, as well as a bibliography and an index at the end. But the book has a second possibility. At the end of each chapter are discussion questions and a Bible study on a passage in the Jewish and Christian Scriptures. These can be used

---

18. Yuk Shuen Wong and Paul Pearce, "Factors Contributing to Healthy Aging," *BC Psychologist*, Vol. 3, Issue 2 (2014), pp. 11-12.

for individual study, but most naturally they could be used for group discussion. In that case the members of the group, for example, who are committed to a nine- or ten-week study could read the chapters in advance of the meeting and discuss the contents, or do the Bible discussion study when they meet. The Bible studies are not "this is what the Bible says" but discovery studies with questions to get you into the text for yourself, discovering useful life application. So — enjoy!

PART ONE

Calling

....

1

Reframing Retirement

Two weeks is about the ideal length of time to retire.

Alex Comfort[1]

Retirement is . . . not in the language of the Christian.

James M. Houston[2]

I have a serious proposal to make: We should work until we die. I realize that this sounds outrageous to people who have been longing for "freedom fifty-five," are planning on getting out of the rat race just as soon as they can, have just been laid off or given an early retirement exit package, and are now looking forward to a life of leisure, playing or consuming their way to death. But I am serious.

The Christian and Jewish Bible know nothing of what we call retirement except one obscure reference in Numbers 8:23-25, where the Levites were to retire at age fifty. Perhaps it is a great idea for religious leaders to retire at fifty and spend their senior years mentoring younger men and women. Perhaps there are reasons for this

---

1. Quoted in Dwight Hervey Small, *When Christians Retire: Finding Your Purpose in the Bonus Years* (Kansas City, MO: Beacon Hill Press, 2000), p. 5.
2. James M. Houston and Michael Parker, *A Vision for the Aging Church: Renewing Ministry for and by Seniors* (Downers Grove, IL: IVP Academic, 2011), p. 23.

strange, isolated reference to retirement, since people in Bible times rarely lived to what we call "old age." They did, however, work until they died. In an agrarian society with people living in extended families, there was always work for older people to do, even if it was done with less energy, including helping with the preparation of meals, getting water, and assisting in the care of grandchildren. In much of the developing world, this is still the case. But with increased life expectancy,[3] meaning that many people can live twenty or thirty years after retiring from their career, and with the advent of the industrial and information society, many people plan to retire from work around sixty-five. Some people dream of early retirement at fifty-five. But then what? Certainly, retirement is changing.

The Changing Face of Retirement

In their book *Age Wave,* Ken Dychtwald and Joe Flower describe how the old way of retirement has changed:

> We are witnessing the end of yesterday's retirement, with grandpa asleep on the porch, the gold watch the company gave him ticking in his vest pocket, and his friends coming over later to go fishing or play cards or checkers. Later life is rapidly becoming a time when you do not stop working completely, but instead shift gears to part-time, seasonal, or occasional work, mixed with productive and involved leisure activities.[4]

3. A decade ago, these were the statistics: "For a 65-year-old couple today, there is a one-in-four chance that one of them will reach 97 years of age, and a one-in-two chance that one will reach the age of 92. Today the average Canadian man lives to 78 and the average Canadian woman to 82." Fidelity Investments, Viewpoint-Retirement Issues Consumer Research Report, 2003 and World Health Organization, www3.who.int, 2003, quoted in *How Will You Spend the Rest of Your Life* (BMO Financial Group). As life expectancy is climbing for older people, however, it is sadly declining for younger people.

4. Quoted in Zalman Schachter-Shalomi, *From Age-ing to Sage-ing: A Profound New Vision of Growing Older* (New York: Grand Central Publishing, 1995), pp. 207-8.

The surrounding culture in the north and west of the globe gives a complicated message on extending our work life. I have two books on my shelves. One is titled *Joy at Work*. The other has the title *The Joy of Not Working*. A couple profiled in *The Vancouver Sun* say, "Our goal would be to use the next 20 to 25 years of healthy living to do what we want. We just haven't been able to figure out what that means, except we know it means as little work as possible and a warm climate. We don't plan to leave an inheritance to anyone."[5] Essentially this secular approach wants no work, no health challenges, no commitments, and no generosity. There are other double messages.

Older people need to step down, we are told, to make room for younger people in professions, trades, and education. But at the same time, older people are asked to keep working in order to contribute to government pension plans to avoid the huge financial "tsunami" looming on the horizon: pension and health costs for a massively expanding senior population. A thousand Canadians and ten thousand Americans turn sixty-five every day. By the year 2016 there will be in Canada more people over the age of sixty-five than children under the age of fourteen.[6] With society becoming increasingly high tech and workplaces using ever more sophisticated technology, aging people, especially those in tech fields, feel they cannot keep up with young men and women who grew up with iPads on their high chairs. But what are they to do? Few people want to work for nothing (with a consequent loss of volunteerism). But as I will soon show, it is not "for nothing." The truth of the matter is that retirement is a relatively recent creation.

Inventing Non-work

Retirement was introduced during the late nineteenth and early twentieth centuries. In the Western world there were no pensions

5. Andrew Allentuck, *Financial Post*, September 7, 2013, quoted in http://www.vancouversun.com/business/Frugal+couple+want+year+plus+retirement/8882784/story.html (accessed July 10, 2014).

6. Statistics Canada, quoted in *How Will You Spend the Rest of Your Life?* (BMO Financial Group).

until recently, and on average people retired "about three years before death."[7] Most worked into their seventies and died shortly after retiring. If poor health required them to stop working earlier, they would be cared for by their families. George Vaillant shows that in the late twentieth century, "the average number of years of retirement prior to death increased from 3 to almost 15 years."[8] So things have radically changed.

The first country to institute formal retirement was Germany in 1889. The official retirement age varies from country to country, ranging from fifty to seventy. In some countries the official age is being raised, not lowered, as older workers are needed to contribute to the tax base rather than drawing from the diminishing pool of pension resources. Greater wealth allows some people to purchase additional years of leisure.

At the other end of the economic spectrum, the financial crisis of 2008 and the malaise that has followed — which appears to be substantially the "new normal" — is forcing people to keep working. A recent article in *The Vancouver Sun*, based on a survey of Canadians, shows that 40 percent of baby boomers in British Columbia (born between 1946 and 1964) are working past retirement age, and 84 percent say they don't plan ever to retire. Why? The reasons are complex. First, they want to remain mentally active. Second, they want the social interaction that work provides. But a full 39 percent say it is a financial necessity. Interviewed boomers say they did not save enough to retire comfortably, that they started thinking about retirement too late, that they have had a poor return on their investments, and a downturn in the economy has affected them. Significantly, almost a third of baby boomers in Canada expect to carry some form of debt into retirement.[9]

7. George E. Vaillant, *Aging Well* (New York: Little, Brown, 2002), p. 222.

8. Vaillant, *Aging Well*, p. 223.

9. "Navigating the Retirement Landscape," *The Vancouver Sun* (June 17, 2014), section A3. While this book does not offer financial advice to prepare for retirement it is appropriate to mention that income after retirement can come from government pension plans, pension plans associated with the organization one has worked for, private savings, and investments. Some fairly sophisticated formulae have been developed to estimate how much one needs to put aside during one's working years

The Negative and Positive Faces of Retirement

Most studies show that retirement is seen negatively if some people are forced to retire before they wish, if they retire because a pre-existing health challenge requires they stop working, or if they have insufficient resources to maintain themselves should they end their career. Some people retire because, as one mortgage manager summarized, "It was no longer fun." Weariness can set in. The pressure seems always to be ramping up, not down. My brother, who worked in a high-tech field, said, "I could no longer keep up with the younger men and women." But the elongation of life has brought about new seasons of life, often unsought. Joan Chittister comments, "In an age when two out of every five workers are forced to stop working earlier than planned, the disorientation has all the characteristics of a social epidemic."[10]

In contrast, Vaillant proposes that retirement can be a rewarding if four things are done. First, retirees should replace their work mates with another social network. Second, they must rediscover how to play. Third, they must cultivate creativity. So Vaillant notes, "Monet did not begin his water lily panels until 76. Benjamin Franklin invented bifocals at 78. Leopold Stokowski signed a six-year recording contract at 94, and Grandma Moses was still painting at 100." Fourth, says Vaillant, they should continue lifelong learning.[11] But what does retirement mean?

For some retirement means moving from full-time to part-time work, or moving from one kind of employment to another. For other people, retirement means taking up a hobby or investing a lot of time in leisure activities. What follows for some people is a life of institutionalized sloth — continuous golf, travelling, driving an RV around North America, and becoming a couch potato before the

---

to be able to live for a reasonable number of years in retirement before death. This is usually calculated from actuarial tables. Some of these calculations show that up to 35 percent of one's salary needs to be put aside, something that rarely happens, which is why so many retired people go back to work, if they can.

10. Joan Chittister, *The Gift of Years: Growing Older Gracefully* (Katonah, NY: Bluebridge, 2008), p. 9.

11. Vaillant, *Aging Well*, pp. 224, 238-39.

television set. Many people upon retirement experience something which is medically described as "delayed postretirement disorientation syndrome accompanied by depression and dysfunction."[12] Tragically, some people, especially men for whom work can be their whole life, die shortly after retiring.

There is no doubt that retirement is a challenge. A married woman describes her husband's retirement this way: "twice as much husband and half as much money." Money is an issue. Not surprisingly, the first wave of resources to help people with retirement — seminars and "how-to-retire with a great lifestyle" books — focused on money. But there is much more than money involved. It is to these that we must turn to reframe our approach to retirement. Reframing means looking at things in a new way, shifting our "attitude about a situation from pessimistic to optimistic," says Lewis Richmond.[13] Just what that involves is what now needs to be explored.

Reframing Retirement

First, retirement, whether voluntary or involuntary, is a useful shock. It is a trauma that can produce a re-evaluation of one's life. Eugene Bianchi explains, "This apparently negative challenge may be just the thing necessary to dislocate rigid, ingrained patterns of behavior. Painful self-assessment sometimes gives way to new insights about creative uses of time and energy for private enjoyment and social enrichment."[14] The questions raised by retirement can become the most important self-assessment tools for the rest of your life: What have I really done with my life up to now? What contribution to family, neighbor, to the world, and the environment do I still want to make? What is the meaning of my life? What am I actually living for? What is most important in my life?

Second, retirement (in the formal sense) can become a time of

---

12. Small, *When Christians Retire*, pp. 22-23.

13. Lewis Richmond, *Aging as a Spiritual Practice: A Contemplative Guide to Growing Older and Wiser* (New York: Gotham Books, 2012), p. 57.

14. Bianchi, *Aging as a Spiritual Journey* (Eugene, OR: Wipf and Stock, 2011), p. 191.

significant personal growth. The growth can be intellectual, social, relational, and spiritual. Bianchi describes this possibility noting the importance of work: "Considerable potential for growth in middle age resides in a person's attitudes toward work. Whether manual or intellectual, work is the mode by which people express and define themselves in the world."[15]

Third, retirement can open up possibilities of work, voluntary or remunerated, that better fits one's gifts, talents, personality, and life experience. Bianchi speaks of this as turning our working life into something more than a mere career, to a religious experience, something which he calls a contemplative approach to work.[16] In the next chapter we will refer to this as "calling."

Fourth, retirement can become a critical time to re-evaluate one's vocation. Essentially, calling provides meaning and purpose in one's life. We do not retire from our calling even if we have retired from a career. "Such work," says Bianchi, "knows no retirement day; loss of such work is the loss of vocation, depriving one of values and meaning."[17]

Fifth, formal retirement can become a time when we can make a transition, as Zalman Schachter-Shalomi describes it, from age-ing to sage-ing.[18] The potential of mentoring the next generation — in the workplace, in the family, in the church or synagogue — opens up possibilities for older people to become elders in the traditional and biblical sense of people noted for wisdom and experience who can be sought for advice, help, support, and direction. "As an alternative to retirement, mentoring enables older workers to remain in the workplace as trainers of younger workers," notes this Jewish rabbi.[19]

An immense longitudinal study of adult development undertaken by Harvard University, tracking people down over their entire lifespan, has made some important discoveries. Key to this, as Vaillant notes, is generativity, which he describes as "taking care of the next generation" and "investing in forms of life and work that

15. Bianchi, *Aging as a Spiritual Journey*, p. 60.
16. Bianchi, *Aging as a Spiritual Journey*, p. 62.
17. Bianchi, *Aging as a Spiritual Journey*, p. 157.
18. Schachter-Shalomi, *From Age-ing to Sage-ing*.
19. Schachter-Shalomi, *From Age-ing to Sage-ing*, p. 207.

will outlive the self."[20] This means that the old are put on earth to nurture the young. The fact that this involves the reversal of the normal family structure is radical: instead of the young looking after the old, the old are to look after the young, caring for them, teaching them, nurturing them, and learning from them. Psalm 92 is titled a Psalm "for the Sabbath Day" and thereby invites us, through putting aside our everyday work and pressures, to reflect on what life is all about, especially how we are to live with God in our senior years. Psalm 92:14 says that the righteous "will still bear fruit in old age, they will stay fresh and green."

There Is Work after Work

Scripture from Genesis to Revelation affirms that work is a critical part of what it means to be a human being in the image of God. This is one of the reasons why I argue that we should work until we die. In 1 Thessalonians 4:9-12 and 2 Thessalonians 3:6-13, the apostle Paul was dealing with the poor work ethic in the churches he served. Some people thought that working in this world was not important or meaningful, so they avoided it as much as possible and became busybodies or wanted to spend their time "doing ministry" since this had, so they thought, eternal consequences. Undoubtedly in the church today we have the same problem, but we must first try to understand what work is, and then why it is so important.

There are many complicated definitions of work but the simplest is this: work is energy expended *purposively* — whether it be manual, mental, or both, and regardless of whether it is or not remunerated. When we play, we may be expending energy, but it is not purposeful.[21]

---

20. Vaillant, *Aging Well*, pp. 114-15.

21. Miroslav Volf defines work this way: "Work is honest, purposeful, and methodologically specified social activity whose primary goal is the creation of products or states of affairs that can satisfy the needs of working individuals or their co-creatures, or (if primarily an end in itself) activity that is necessary in order for acting individuals to satisfy their needs apart from the need of the activity itself." Miroslav Volf, *Work in the Spirit: Toward a Theology of Work* (New York: Oxford University Press, 1991), pp. 10-11.

We are not making a service or a product. Often, however, work and play overlap, as is certainly the case with little children, for whom work is play and play is work. Often this overlap is witnessed in our everyday language, such as "I play the piano" or "I am playing hockey." To open up the theme of this chapter, let me introduce you to some people who are officially "retired" but are still working. I have changed the names, but they are all real people.

Sam retired from being a Boeing 747 captain and has taken up repairing boats, something he had always loved to do. Eleanor was an executive with a major financial firm and is now an administrator in a church. Ed was a high school design technology teacher (the new name for "shop teacher") who, upon retirement, fixes things in people's homes as a volunteer, especially widows and the poor. Linda was a hospital chaplain who now visits people in seniors' homes. Darrell was a school counselor but now works as a volunteer with an organization that connects people inside prison with people outside prison. Melinda worked as a secretary but now serves as voluntary secretary for a couple of not-for-profit organizations. Lee worked all his life in vegetable oil production but on retirement uses his vast experience to head up an organization that is reinventing cooking oil as well as serving with the UN, advising countries on how to add high protein to their diets. Sandra was a homemaking mom who has, in a sense, never retired — except to say to her newly retired husband, "I am not making lunches" — who not only maintains their much smaller condo suite but does a lot of the driving for and personal care of her grandchildren.

James was an academic and, after officially retiring, continues to teach part-time and travels to visit his former students and "nudge them along" in their own growth. Gwen was a high level administrator in a school district and now offers her service free of charge to a new experimental educational program. Dan worked in the tech department of a large manufacturing company and now runs a small farm, something he always wanted to do. Lydia used to be hostess and manager of a restaurant but now caters for funerals in a local funeral home (part-time pay) and church social events (voluntary). Alvin was a farmer; after his son took over the farm he continues to "help out" around the farm while they live in a smaller house nearby. *The Globe and Mail* recently published an obituary for Ben Etkin, a Canadian aeronautical engineer who in 1970 with his slide rule (pre-computer) helped save the doomed and crippled Apollo 13 flight. The article noted that "he never really retired." Even in the retirement home he figured out a way to help a friend with Parkinson's reduce the degree of movement with a sleeve he designed.[22] Every one of these people would say they are doing something they love. They all have more leisure time since they retired, but they are all working, some for remuneration but others as volunteers. And it is good.

So why should we work until we die whether or not the work is remunerated? And will we indeed even work after we die in the new resurrected life in the new heaven and new earth? I will take up the latter question of work in the next life later. But let us start with the life we have now. Here are some reasons.

First, we are made to work. Work is part of our God-imaging dignity as human beings. We are made, as Genesis tells us, to be icons or reflections of the divine being. Staying with Scripture, we find in the seminal passage in Genesis, the first book of the Bible, that being a God-reflecting being involves two things. We are made as relational beings, "male and female in his image" (Gen. 1:27), built for community. The reason for this is that God is a relational being dwelling in the love and service communion of Father, Son, and Spirit. So people are beings in communion. And at the core of human dignity is relationship.

But the other dimension of human God-likeness is equally important. God is a worker.[23] God is still working, as Jesus says (John 5:17). And we are made like God in that we work. We were given

---

22. Judy Stoffman, "Mighty Brain Helped Avert Apollo 13 Tragedy," *Globe and Mail* (July 24, 2014): S10.

23. Throughout the Bible, we see different images of God as a worker, namely, shepherd (Ps. 23), potter (Jer. 18:6), physician (Matt. 8:16), teacher (Ps. 143:10), vineyard-dresser (Isa. 5:1-7), etc. God is as active and creative today — creating, sustaining, redeeming, and consummating — as God was when this five-billion-light-year universe was begun. See Robert Banks, *God the Worker: Journeys into the Mind, Heart and Imagination of God* (Valley Forge, PA: Judson Press, 1994).

dominion or rule over everything except ourselves and told to "work [the earth] and take care of it" (Gen. 1:26; 2:15). We do this in everything from agriculture to genetic engineering, from accounting to graphic art. And the reason is simply this: God invites human beings to enter his ongoing work of designing, communicating, creating, sustaining, and organizing (we could add dozens of verbs and nouns in Scripture that describe God at work). Joan Chittister puts it this way: "As long as we breathe we have responsibility for the co-creation of the world, for the good of the human race."[24] Of course work is not easy, and ever since the first big problem in the world, commonly called the fall, there have been thorns and thistles (Gen. 3:1-24). The workplace has become complicated, politicized, and all too often just plain hard. And we ourselves experience what God said to Adam, "sweat on our brows" (read "stress"). Since work was given before the fall into sin, it is essentially good, even though there has been a problem. Subsequently, work has been substantially healed since Christ has largely reversed the curse. [25]

Second, work is good for the world. The Bible opens with a double vision: God at work speaking, designing, and crafting, and God-imaging human beings mandated to "work (the garden) and take care of it" (Gen. 2:15). Contrary to what most people think, the world was not made for human beings; people were made for the world. We care for creation in spectacular ways — town planning, serving in government, sending a rocket into space, and splicing a gene — as well as the most mundane — collecting the garbage, keeping financial accounts, styling someone's hair, changing a di-

---

24. Chittister, *The Gift of Years*, p. 53.

25. Despite the pervasiveness of the effects of sin, God in Christ has redeemed the entire created order (note the repeated use of the words "all things" in Col. 1:15-20 in regard to both creation and redemption). Apart from humans, creation also waits for the day when it will be set free from bondage (Rom. 8:19-23). The cosmic scope of God's redemption means that everything affected by sin and the curse can be redeemed, including human work. God redeems work through his church when by the power of the Holy Spirit, his people bring God's presence (Matt. 5:16-17) and godly values (Prov. 16:11; Matt. 5:13-17; Prov. 20:10; Amos 5:10-12) into the workplace. Obviously, unethical, immoral, and exploitative practices have no place in God's kingdom and purposes.

aper, putting a meal on the table, and selling paint. All of it "keeps stable" (says an ancient document) "the fabric of the world." So work is good for creation, or should be. But work is also good for us.

Third, work is good for us. Work does several good things for us: it gets us out of ourselves. In his classic book *Life Together*, Dietrich Bonhoeffer speaks of the therapeutic value of work (that is my word, not his): "Work plunges men [sic] into the world of things. The Christian steps out of the world of brotherly encounter into the world of impersonal things, the 'it'; and this new encounter frees him for objectivity; for the 'it'-world is only an instrument in the hand of God for the purification of Christians from all self-centeredness and self-seeking." Bonhoeffer continues, "Work [is] a means of liberation from himself."[26]

Through work we express gifts and talents. In the end we are accountable to God as to whether we have used the talents and resources with which he has entrusted us.[27] Work also enables us to provide for ourselves and our loved ones (2 Thess. 3:7-10). And work facilitates generosity when we can share our excess with the needy and pay our taxes which, by and large, is a way of loving our neighbours (Eph. 4:28). As God delighted in his creation (Gen. 1:31), humans too find fulfillment when they do good work. Hence we acknowledge that our enjoyment of work is also a gift from God (Eccles. 3:13; 5:18). So work is good for us. But it is also good for others.

Fourth, work is a practical way of loving our neighbor. The original Greek word for "ministry" is simply "service." Ministry is all the ways we serve God and others, ways about which God says "it is good" (Gen. 1:31). Some daily work is an obvious ministry — counselling, pastoring, preaching, teaching, and healing. Most good work is behind the scenes — connecting people through the Internet,

---

26. Dietrich Bonhoeffer, *Life Together*, trans. John W. Doberstein (New York: Harper and Row, 1954), p. 70.

27. At the culmination of God's purposes when Jesus comes again, Christians will be judged not only for their work that is directly related to evangelism and the church but also for their faithfulness as stewards with the resources and responsibilities that God has given them: material resources, gifts, training, and skills (Matt. 25:31-36). The judgment criterion puts into perspective God's expectations of us on a broader scale and thus validates our present human work in various capacities.

getting the data into the right bank, conveying a title, and lubricating the gears of a machine — but all these nonreligious works are just as important in God's eyes. This is especially true for lab technicians, researchers, and people in manufacturing who cannot see the neighbor they are serving. When did you last think of going to work (or looking for work if you are unemployed) as "going into the ministry"? But all good work is a practical way of loving our fellow human beings, something which all of Scripture and Jesus in particular calls us to do. In speaking of business in particular, the theologian Kenneth Kantzer puts it this way: "By creation, human beings are social beings, never intended to live alone. Because of our social nature, we are specialized (each person is, in one sense, unique), interdependent, and, therefore, necessarily dependent on exchange. Exchange is built into our very nature."[28]

We do not retire from loving our neighbors, though we may find other ways of doing so than the remunerated work to which we have given ourselves in the various careers of our lifetime.

Fifth, work participates in the spreading of the kingdom of God. The kingdom is the active, *shalom*-bringing, life-giving rule of God in the world in which we can participate through work. The kingdom is holistic, comprehensive. We can derive an idea of the holistic nature of God's mission by looking at Jesus' ministry on earth. He has rightly been called the kingdom of God in person. He not only preached the "gospel of the kingdom of God" (Luke 9:2; 10:11); he embodied the kingdom. He met people's physical needs but also ministered to their emotional, psychological, and physical needs. He worked at his carpentry (Mark 6:3), fed the five thousand (Matt. 14:15-21), healed the sick and cast out demons (Matt. 8:16), raised Lazarus from the dead (John 11:43-44), and washed his disciples' feet (John 13:4-5). The kingdom of God is not just spiritual: it is personal, social, political, economic, and cosmic. Most good work in this world is a way to extend the kingdom of God and to bring *shalom* to people and creation. The distinction often made between

---

28. Kenneth S. Kantzer, "God Intends His Precepts to Transform Society," in Richard C. Chewning, ed., *Biblical Principles & Business* (Colorado Springs: NavPress, 1989), p. 24.

spiritual work (sometimes expressed as "kingdom work") and so-called "secular" work is both unbiblical and harmful. Gospel work and societal work are interdependent, and together they fulfill the prayer taught by Jesus, "Thy kingdom come." This implies that all human work that embodies kingdom values and serves the kingdom goal can be regarded as kingdom work.

Sixth, work is the main context in which we grow spiritually. It is tragically true that some people in retirement give themselves to continuous non-work and play their way to the grave. Is that good for them spiritually? Usually people who win the lottery or inherit vast estates and no longer work shrink spiritually. Eugene Peterson, the well-known translator of *The Message,* affirms the centrality of work in spiritual formation: "I'm prepared to contend that the primary location for spiritual formation is the workplace."[29] How can this be true?

Besides the insightful comment by Dietrich Bonhoeffer above, all the issues we face at work are invitations to grow as persons and persons with souls: failure, success, succession, delegation, frustration, competition. In all probability our major vulnerability, sometimes called our Achilles' heel, usually is manifested mostly at work. It could be our need to be needed, our need for approval, or our need to be in control. And at precisely the point of our vulnerability, we have an opportunity to grow. As Alvin Ung and I show in *Taking Your Soul to Work,* the seven deadly sins — pride, greed, lust, sloth, gluttony, anger, and envy — are remarkably matched to the ninefold fruit of the Spirit (Gal. 5:22-26).[30] This means that we are hardwired by the Creator to find God and grow at precisely the point of our need. Indeed, every need is a kind of prayer. Prayer itself comes naturally as we work and is the major way in which we access the presence and the provision of God for growth and help. Even the simple cry "Help" not only accesses the infinite resources of God but even more importantly connects us with God.

29. Eugene H. Peterson, *Christ Plays in Ten Thousand Places: A Conversation in Spiritual Theology* (Grand Rapids: Eerdmans, 2005), p. 127.

30. R. Paul Stevens and Alvin Ung, *Taking Your Soul to Work: Overcoming the Nine Deadly Sins of the Workplace* (Grand Rapids: Eerdmans, 2010).

Finally, work prepares us for the life to come. The eschatological (end times) vision in the Old Testament is that of humanity at work.[31] This picture is completed for us in the New Testament. Our final destination as Christians is a glorified material destination described as a new heaven and a new earth (Rev. 21–22; Isaiah 65). We will not be "saved souls" in "heaven" but fully resurrected persons in the new heaven and new earth. The redeemed community will inhabit this new creation in their glorified bodies (1 Cor. 15; Phil. 3:21). They will bring their cultures and their ethnic and linguistic diversities.[32] All of this strongly suggests that there will be continuity with our present existence, which will undergo a dramatic, transformative, and cathartic renewal. In some ways which we do not fully understand, our human work and labor will surely find a way into the new creation (Rev. 14:13). It is not just our spiritual work and our spiritual life that will endure and that matter to God, but all work and life undertaken with faith, hope, and love.[33] The kings of the earth bring their glories into the holy city (Rev. 21:24), and thus the transfigured creation will be embellished by the deeds of Christians, deeds that "follow them" (Rev. 14:13). So our labor in the Lord is "not in vain" (1 Cor. 15:58).

So there is good news from the message of the Bible. In the new heaven and earth, we will be fully human beings who, along with continuous worship, amazing relationships, and awesome experience, will enjoy work as we never did in this life. Hidden talents will be expressed. Creativity that was on the "back burner" for much of our earthly work life will find expression. And our unique and particular giftedness will find expression in a community of giving and receiving, an exchange which, as some have imaginatively suggested, would be business without the passing of money. The last book of the Bible pictures the people of God in these words: "They will rule [read "work"] with [Christ] age after age after age" (Rev. 22:5).[34] In a profound sense, the work we do in this life is a

---

31. Amos 9:13; Mic. 4:3ff.; Isa. 11:1; Hos. 2:18-23.

32. Rev. 5:9; 21:24, 26.

33. 1 Cor. 13:13; 1 Thess. 1:2-3.

34. Eugene H. Peterson, *The Message* (Colorado Springs: NavPress, 2002), p. 2264.

preparation for work we will do forever even if there is no direct correspondence with the actual deed, substance, or subject of our daily work. The giftedness we bring to work, the way we actually work, and, most important of all, for whom we work, will all carry over into the finest workplace in the universe with the best working conditions imaginable.

So why would you *not* want to work until you die? It will be part of your calling, from which you will never retire. But if work is only part of our calling, what is the rest? And how do we go about finding our calling for the rest of our lives? To that subject we must now turn.

Personal or Group Study: Proverbs; 1 Thessalonians 3–4

Personal Reflection:
Review your family story on the issue of work and retirement. What did your parents and grandparents do as they reached their senior years? What was their attitude toward work before and after they ceased remunerated work or, in the case of homemaking mothers, after the major homemaking responsibilities ceased?

Group Discussion:
Imagine for a moment that you have so much money now that you will never have to work again. Would that be a good thing spiritually?

Bible Study:
Read Proverbs 6:6-11; 10:26; 13:4; 15:19; 21:25-26
1. Proverbs paints an almost humorous picture of the "sluggard" with a few deft strokes. Describe the inner attitude and outer effects of the sluggard in relation to life's responsibilities.
2. Sloth, one of the seven deadly sins elaborated by the church, has been defined as the evasion of duty, when ease seems sweet and when the very thought of labor is troublesome. What is so wrong about doing nothing, or as little as possible, as a way of life?

3. Derek Kidner describes the challenge of hiring a sluggard: "He will not begin things. . . . He will not finish things. . . . He will not face things. . . . Consequently he is *restless* (13:4; 21:25, 26) with unsatisfied desire; *helpless* in the face of the tangle of his affairs, which are like a 'hedge of thorns' (15:19); and *useless* — expensively (18:9) and exasperatingly (10:26) — to anyone who must employ him."[35] When in your experience have you encountered such people?

4. Reflect on your own work-rest history. Are you inclined to overwork, underwork, or live a fairly balanced life of work and rest?

5. Scripture encourages us to take one day in seven for complete rest and cessation of work (the Sabbath; Exod. 20:8-11). Could retirement be considered as an extended Sabbath and therefore a good thing? Why or why not? What would be the value in a person taking a Sabbath year after formal retirement as a season to discern his or her calling for the rest of his or her life?

6. It has been said that there is no word for retirement in the Christian vocabulary. Do you agree or disagree? Why?

7. Many people give the "first half" of their life to becoming successful and then, often in what is called a mid-life transition, seek to do something significant with the second half. Is this a good way to approach growing older? If so why? If not why not?

Read 1 Thessalonians 4:9-12; 2 Thessalonians 3:6-13

8. One of the problems the apostle Paul faced in the churches he served was a poor work ethic. Some people thought that working in this world was not important or meaningful, and so they avoided it as much as possible and became busybodies or wanted to spend their time "doing ministry" since this had, so they thought, eternal consequences. Where in the contemporary church do you see this same problem?

9. Why does Paul say believers should work? (Note: other pas-

35. Derek Kidner, *Proverbs* (Downers Grove, IL: InterVarsity Press, 1972), pp. 42-43.

sages in Paul's correspondence give some additional reasons for believers to work hard: Eph. 4:28; Col. 3:22–4:1.)

10. Jesus summed up the law in the two commandments of loving God and neighbor. In what ways could your own life be a way of loving God and your neighbors through work even if that work is not remunerated?

11. What are the challenges and advantages of releasing a generation of aging people to work as volunteers in the church and the world?

"Man was placed in Paradise . . . that he would till the land not in servile labor but with a spiritual pleasure befitting his dignity."

St. Augustine[36]

---

36. Augustine, *The Literal Meaning of Genesis*, vol. 2, no. 42, Ancient Christian Writers, trans. John Hammond Taylor (New York: Newman Press, 1982), p. 46.

2

The Immensely Important Matter of Late-Life Calling

It is impossible to live through the evening of life in accordance with the programmes appropriate for the morning, since what has great importance then will have very little now, and the truth of the morning will be the error of the evening.

Carl Jung[1]

In any moment we meet the call of God anew, and, hence, in every moment it is as it were "just setting out."

Karl Barth[2]

Here are two people trying to figure out what to do with the rest of their lives: Frank and Nathaniel. Frank is retiring from being a CEO of a manufacturing company. At his retirement dinner he reflects on the future. He hopes, he says, to keep his hand in the company, doing some consulting on a limited basis. But he also wants to take up some entrepreneurial activity on a part-time basis. Now that he will be substantially free from the necessity of working for a living, and with his considerable assets solidly in place, he wants to do what

---

1. Carl Jung, in Paul Tournier, *Learn to Grow Old* (Louisville: Westminster John Knox Press, 1991), p. 11.
2. Karl Barth, *Church Dogmatics* III/4 (Edinburgh: T&T Clark, 1961), pp. 607-18.

he has always dreamed of (but never felt he had time for while on the corporate treadmill) — to work in ministry in the local church. Perhaps some of his work will be in the Third World, to which he hopes to travel annually. He and his wife hope that retirement will give them the opportunity to finally get "their life into a single, seamless, integrated whole."

At the dinner honoring Nathaniel, he was given accolades for his service as senior sales manager of a paper company. But at that dinner Nathaniel made a stunning announcement: he plans to abruptly change the course of his life. He has one simple plan for the coming years: he wants to learn how to die. To that end he wants fewer possessions; for, as Cicero put it, "Can anything be more absurd in the traveler than to increase his luggage as he nears his journey's end?" He has, he says, much reading he needs to do. He hopes to write some reminiscences for his children. And he wants to learn the art of contemplative and intercessory prayer. He intends to begin every day with these words from a prayer by John Baillie:

> Forbid, O Lord, that my thoughts today should be wholly occupied with the world's passing show. Seeing that in Thy loving-kindness Thou hast given me the power to lift my mind to the contemplation of things unseen and eternal, forbid that I should remain content with the things of sense and time. Grant rather that each day may do something so to strengthen my hold upon the unseen world, so to increase my sense of its reality, and so to attach my heart to its holy interests that, as the end of my earthly life draws ever nearer, I may not grow to be part of these fleeting earthly surroundings, but rather grow more and more conformed to the life of the world to come.[3]

If you were present at these two retirement dinners, how would you react? What fears does each person reveal? To which of these two would you turn for advice?

These two examples show the complexity of discovering late-

---

3. Adapted from Gilbert Meilaender, "Mortality," *First Things* 10 (February 1991): 14-21.

life calling. On the one hand, as Carl Jung said in the quotation above, things are different. Aging makes a change in the meaning we are seeking in life. "[W]hat has great importance then will have very little now." On the other hand, there is continuity in one's calling in life even if remunerated work stops. While the calling may continue, the expression of it will change, and perhaps in senior years change radically. Take my own life as an example.

I have been a pastor, a student counselor, a carpenter, a business owner (construction and renovation), a professor, and a self-employed consultant. It looks like I have been confused (and indeed I have had such periods). But my calling is to empower the whole people of God for service in the world, and to care for and love God, my family, and my neighbor, and to make beautiful things to embellish the earth and people. That calling has remained constant even though the *manifestation* of the calling has changed fairly radically. And now, at seventy-eight, I am still trying to find out what I am to do with my life when I finally grow up! So I join you in an exciting journey, a journey of both self-discovery and God-discovery. Karl Barth, in the quotation above, said it better: "In every moment it is as it were 'just setting out.'"

To undertake this journey, we will need first to explore what calling is, including its comprehensiveness, some misunderstanding about calling, the process of discerning calling, what is so good about being called, and, finally, how to function with vocational integrity.

What Is Calling?

By using the word "calling," I am preferring the old word for *vocation*, but they are the same thing.[4] *Voco* and *vocatio* in Latin mean "call" and "calling." Unfortunately, the common English usage of *vocation* has become equated with *occupation*. But there is more to

---

4. Some of the following was first published in R. Paul Stevens, "Vocational Guidance," in Robert Banks and R. Paul Stevens, eds. *The Complete Book of Everyday Life* (Downers Grove, IL: InterVarsity Press, 1997), pp. 1078-85.

vocation than one's occupation, from which one can easily retire through necessity or ill health. By using the word "calling," I am also raising an important point, namely, that while one chooses a career, one is *chosen* for a calling. For there to be a callee, there must be a caller. And the caller is the divine Creator. Even people who do not believe in God, or people who have faiths other than the Jewish or Christian faiths, are called because God calls everyone, whether they know the origin of their calling or not. Often people will say, "I was born for this," "This is what I am meant to be and to do." Os Guinness has written winsomely about this. "When something more than human seeking is needed if seeking is to be satisfied, then calling means that seekers themselves are sought."[5] That said, our Creator seeks and calls every human being and does so in three ways, as expounded in the New Testament Scriptures.

First, we are called to belong to God. Our seeking God longs for communion with his creature, and we long for communion with our Maker, even if that longing gets suppressed or diverted by other longings and idols. "You have made us for yourself," said St. Augustine, "and our heart is restless until it rests in you."[6] According to the figurative, poetic account of creation in the first book of the Bible, God placed Adam and Eve in a sanctuary garden where they could commune with him 24/7. God is pictured as walking in the garden in the cool of the day to spend time with his beloved creatures. In the New Testament we discover that one of the purposes of God's sending his Son, Jesus, to Earth was not merely to recruit workers in God's grand schemes for the renewal of creation and people, but to have communion with God. According to 1 Corinthians 1:7, "God . . . has called you into fellowship with his son, Jesus Christ our Lord." This part of our calling does not change with age, though as I will show in the section on spirituality, it is deepened and intensified. So belonging to God comes before doing God's work. But there is another dimension to calling.

5. Os Guinness, *The Call: Finding and Fulfilling the Central Purpose of Your Life* (Nashville: Word Publishing, 1998), p. 10.

6. Augustine, *Confessions,* trans. Henry Chadwick (Oxford: Oxford University Press, 1998), p. 3.

Second, we are called to live righteously. Righteousness in Scripture is not the same as piety. Righteousness is living in right relationship with God and people. So this second dimension of calling is a matter of *being,* a way of life. The New Testament uses "call" language to describe being called to a life of love, holiness, freedom, and hope.[7] Does this change with aging? In principle it does not, but in expression we are called to deepen our way of life to become models and examples to the coming generation. The apostle Paul wrote to his protégé Timothy that this young man had observed "my way of life" (2 Tim. 3:10). Parents and grandparents teach mainly by example, and the challenging thing to all education, formal or informal, is, as Jesus once observed, that it is essentially a process of imitation. "Students are not above their teacher, but all who are fully trained will be *like* their teacher" (Luke 6:40, emphasis mine). We will explore this more deeply in the chapters on the vices and virtues of aging. But there is another dimension of calling, and it is the only one most people associate with their vocation.

Third, we are called to service, to do God's work and to enter into God's service in both the church and the world. This involves gifts, talents, ministries, occupations, roles, work, and mission.[8] And in this way we fulfill the human vocation to take care of the earth, to develop the potential of creation, and to care for people as mandated in the foundational calling passage of Genesis 1:27-28. It is here that there is the most change and the most misunderstanding about change that takes place, as people face the second half or the third third of life. The misunderstanding is that people of faith who have given the lion's share of their life to what they call a "secular" job want to do something that has lasting, even eternal significance. So they want to "go into the ministry" — either full-time, by obtaining a seminary education and then getting ordained, or part-time, by becoming a volunteer in a religious organization. There is, of course, no problem with this if this is a genuine leading of God and suitable to one's gifts and talents (though sometimes it is not), but there is a problem if such people think that they are moving from secular

---

7. 1 Cor. 7:15; Gal. 5:13; Eph. 4:4; Col. 3:15; 1 Thess. 4:7; 2 Tim. 1:9.
8. Exod. 19:6; Isa. 41:2; 42:6; Matt. 4:21; Mark 3:13-14; Eph. 4:1; 1 Pet. 2:9-10.

work to doing God's work. As we noted in the last chapter, we can be doing "God's work" in a myriad of good occupations in the world, entering into God's continuing creativity, God's sustaining work, God's transformative work, and God's consummating (finishing) work.

In the twelfth century Walter Hilton, an Augustinian canon, received a letter from a businessman who wanted to leave his secular occupation and go into the monastery. This kind of thing seems to happen frequently at the "half time" period of life, especially for men. Hilton replied in his "Letter to a Layman." He told the man, in effect, not to leave his employment but to go deeper, to combine the life of activity with the life of contemplation, to join Martha and Mary, two archetypes in the Gospel story, one given to activity and one to contemplation.[9] Hilton wrote,

> You ought to mingle the works of an active life with spiritual endeavors of a contemplative life, and then you will do well. For you should at certain times be busy with Martha in the ordering and care of your household, children, employees, tenants, or neighbors. . . . At other times you should, with Mary, leave off the busyness of this world and sit down meekly at the feet of our Lord, there to be in prayer, holy thought, and contemplation of him, as he gives you grace.[10]

The loss of vocation in the modern and postmodern world is further indicated by the fact that almost the only people who speak of being called are so-called full-time missionaries and pastors. Clearly we live in a post-vocational age. Without a theology of vocation, we lapse into debilitating alternatives: fatalism (doing what is required by "the forces," or "the powers"); luck (which denies purposefulness in life and reduces our life to a bundle of accidents); karma (which ties performance to future rewards); nihilism (which denies that there is any good end to which the travail

9. Luke 10:38-42.
10. Walter Hilton, *Toward a Perfect Love*, trans. David L. Jeffrey (Portland: Multnomah, 1985), pp. 8-9.

of history might lead); and, the most common alternative today, self-actualization (in which we invent the meaning and purpose of our lives, making us magicians). In contrast, the biblical doctrine of vocation gives the whole of our lives meaning in relation to the sweet summons of a good God.

The complexity of this issue is well illustrated in the two responses to retirement symbolized in the stories of Frank and Nathaniel. But their stories do not expound all the misunderstandings that exist about calling. There are others.

Misunderstanding Calling

So we must start by clearing away some misunderstandings about calling.[11]

First, God does not have a wonderful plan for our lives. He has something far better — a wonderful purpose! For some Christians, concern "to be in the center of God's will" leads to guidance anxiety. A plan, like a blueprint, must be followed in slavish detail, but a purpose is like a fast-flowing stream that carries a boat along and incorporates even mistakes into its ultimate direction. To participate in God's grand purpose of renewing everything in Christ means to oppose evil, to do the work of maintaining a city, to build community, to create systems that bring dignity and value to human life. So John Calvin counsels that believers should "choose those employments which yield the greatest advantage to their neighbors."[12] This does not mean, however, going into the ministry or choosing a Christian service career or a "people" job. With our talents and gifts we can serve our neighbor advantageously even if we do not have direct "people" involvement.

Second, vocation is not the same as remunerated employment. Indeed, we do not need to have remunerated employment to have

11. Some of the following is derived from R. Paul Stevens, "Calling," in Banks and Stevens, *The Complete Book of Everyday Christianity*, pp. 97-102.

12. John Calvin, *Institutes of the Christian Religion*, 2 vols., ed. J. T. McNeill, trans. F. L. Battles (Philadelphia: Westminster, 1960), *Opera*, XLI, p. 300.

vocational contentment. Some fulfill their service to humankind through volunteer work. Occupations, careers, and professions are important parts of our vocation in Christ, but they are not the whole. Calling is comprehensive. According to Scripture, the first human couple was given three full-time jobs, not just one: first, to enjoy full-time communion with God; second, to build community on earth starting with the relationship of male and female; and third, to take care of God's earth (Gen. 2:15) and develop God's creation as coworkers with God (Gen. 4:20-22). While sin marred this threefold human vocation, Christ has reclaimed us for this, and we enjoy substantial redemption until there is complete fulfillment of the human vocation in the New Jerusalem. So work in all its forms is much more than remunerated employment, though that employment may be located primarily in one of the three full-time jobs. Christians are required to seek gainful employment, to meet their own needs (1 Thess. 4:12; 2 Thess. 3:12), and to meet the needs of others (Eph. 4:28). But when we are technically unemployed or retired, we are still caught up in God's all-embracing summons.

Third, calling is not limited to a specifically religious occupation. As reflected in the opening stories, this is where there is the most confusion. Frank seems not to have regarded his work as part of his calling, and now, in retirement, wants to do something he considers significant with his life, such as serving in the developing or majority world and being more involved in the church. A truncated understanding of vocation as merely relating to the Great Commission (Matt. 28:18-20) has resulted in the tragic loss of dignity to persons working in various so-called secular occupations. Thus teachers, lawyers, and doctors have been tacitly placed in a subordinate rank to pastors, evangelists, and missionaries, these last being designated as *ministers*. But the gospel calls us to serve God's purposes in the world through civic, social, political, domestic, and ecclesiastical roles in order to do the work of the Lord.

The big question, however, is, What is "the work *of* the Lord"? The classic definition by J. Campbell White can be easily understood to mean religious or Christian service: "Fame, pleasure, and riches are but husks and ashes in contrast with the boundless and abiding joy of working with God for the fulfilment of his eternal plans. The men who are putting everything into Christ's undertaking are getting out of life its sweetest and most prized rewards."[13] But what is Christ's purpose toward the world, and what is the work of God? Not just church work or cross-cultural mission work. Christ's purpose toward the world is the kingdom of God — God's life-giving, *shalom*-bringing rule in people, society, and all creation. As we have seen in the last chapter, there is no occupation better than another to please God; it doesn't matter whether one is a cobbler or an apostle, washing dishes or preaching. And all good work, in some way, advances the kingdom of God.

In later life, the "doing" may involve a continuation of the same work but at a reduced pace, and possibly with little or no remuneration. Dr. James Houston continues to teach in spiritual theology (though not as intensively) even though he is now in his nineties. The "doing" part of our calling may well involve recovering a hobby that has languished over the years because of the fever pitch of earning a living in younger years. But, warns Paul Tournier, "It is rare for a retired person who has had no other occupation than his work to take up a new activity."[14] All of this suggests the need to prepare for retirement before the actual day, since the "doing" part of our retirement will not be meaningful if it amounts to simply aimless diversions. Without this preparation, many become couch potatoes glued to the TV screen or, if they have the financial means, they take one ocean cruise after another until their have cruised themselves to death.

Friends of mine have successfully prepared for retirement. An obstetrician I know has always enjoyed working in wood, and now in retirement has developed a workshop to make furniture for his children and toys for his grandchildren. Sandra, retired from active parenting, has renewed a long-dormant interest in icon painting.

13. J. Campbell White, "The Layman's Missionary Movement," in *Perspectives on the World Christian Movement*, ed. Ralph D. Winter and Steven C. Hawthorne (Pasadena, CA: William Carey Library, 1981), p. 22, quoted in James M. Houston and Michael Parker, *A Vision for the Aging Church: Renewing Ministry for and by Seniors* (Downers Grove, IL: IVP Academic, 2011), p. 225.

14. Tournier, *Learn to Grow Old*, p. 18.

She took lessons in the art and finds this to be a wonderful expression of her heart and spirit, as well as a service to others. Tournier comments on this special transition for many women: "Almost always the . . . departure of the children, especially of the last child, causes in the mother an emotional crisis much more serious than she expected. . . ."[15] But Sandra prepared for this transition and finds herself newly inspired. Bud was a "people person" at IBM who informally pastored his colleagues and coworkers. When he retired, he started spending time with bicycle couriers in my city and now is their informal pastor. Before a dangerous trip he asked me whether I would conduct his funeral, but he had a word of advice for me. "You'll need to use a large church because all the bicycle couriers in the city will be there."

Generally there is a seed of this new direction already present during the active working years. And the new direction can legitimately be called a "second career."[16] It is distinguished from the first by its freedom, that is, it is taken up because one wants to do it, not because it is required by the demands of a corporation, a profession, a trade, or an organization. Some people take up writing or painting. Others take up gardening or woodworking. How do they discern their calling in this period of transition?

Discovering Late-Life Calling

Extrapolating on this theme of late-life vocational transition in his superb and very personal book on aging, Paul Tournier says:

> In order to make a success of the first phase, which Jung calls the natural life, it is necessary to specialize, to attain a high degree of culture in a restricted field, inevitably at the expense of a broad cultural horizon. The active person allows many of his talents to lie fallow in order to develop a few which are indispensable to his professional and social success. The integration to which Jung

---

15. Tournier, *Learn to Grow Old*, p. 17.
16. See Tournier, "A Second Career," in *Learn to Grow Old*, pp. 122-68.

calls him in the second half of his life, this new advance towards a more complete human fulfillment, involves the reawakening of everything that he has for a long time had to sacrifice to his career.[17]

Here are some specific guidelines to aid in discernment. *First, God guides by investing in our essential motivation.* Mine is to design and build. For others it is to fix or to bring to perfection. For some it is to overcome opposition. Some people are primarily motivated to care for others. Elizabeth O'Connor says "We ask to know the will of God without guessing that his will is written into our very beings."[18] Ralph Mattson and Arthur Miller have devoted themselves to making links between the central motivational thrust and its primary vocational expression in the workplace. Their approach, now systemized in the SIMA test, assumes that (1) God has made us with the capacity to enjoy working and serving in a particular way; (2) what brings joy to us is a powerful indication of what God has designed us to be and do; (3) our central motivating pattern is consistent through life — the boy that nurses a wounded bird at five drives an ambulance at thirty-five.

Both sophisticated and simpler tests are now available to measure interests, natural aptitudes, values, personality type, learning style, and life changes, and many of these tests have been made available in self-help workbooks such as *Naturally Gifted: A Self-Discovery Workbook* by Gordon Jones and Rosemary Jones.[19] These tests help people understand themselves (though they seldom acknowledge that much of the world does not enjoy the luxury of occupational choice or the privilege of a fulfilling career). Since our capacity for self-deception is enormous, the process of knowing ourselves is lifelong. Action-oriented, task-oriented, high-energy people especially need spiritual disciplines to get in touch with themselves. The choice of a career, a marriage partner,

17. Tournier, *Learn to Grow Old*, p. 11.
18. Elizabeth O'Connor, *The Eighth Day of Creation* (Waco, TX: Word, 1971), pp. 14-15.
19. Gordon Jones and Rosemary Jones, *Naturally Gifted: A Self-Discovery Workbook* (Downers Grove, IL: InterVarsity Press, 1993).

or even a role in the church frequently is infused with internal fantasies, a wished-for self that becomes a means of gaining a psychosocial identity. All of this points to the process of vocational guidance as being central, rather than auxiliary, to our life in God.

Second, our gifts and talents are given to us by our Creator, and through these God guides us to serve our neighbor in the world. These gifts and talents normally do not change through our lives, although they may be neglected and brought out of storage in our senior years, often in a hobby or something which could legitimately be called "a second career."

Third, our Creator has given us a personality that does not change substantially during our lifetimes. Some religious people, in explaining their experience of conversion, say things like "God completely changed my personality." Actually what spiritual conversion does is not to change our personalities but to release them from the bondage of sin that stultifies them. The apostle Paul was by nature someone who would beat down opposition and "win." When he became a follower of Christ, his motivation changed from drivenness to gratitude, but his personality did not change. He persisted in overcoming opposition and "winning." I tend toward introversion, but that does not mean I should not be involved in "people work." Just the reverse. It may indicate that I need to be involved in a way that is more evocative and contemplative rather than, say, in direct sales.

Fourth, circumstances significantly shape our sense of calling. God is involved providentially in our lives. We are not a bundle of accidents. So our birth, family background, educational and work experiences, and even our physical and emotional capacities or limitations are a significant part of discovering how we are to discern our calling to belong, be, and do. God is leading through all of the above and the next one to follow.

Finally, God (sometimes) leads directly. To some he speaks orally or through a profound impression in one's imagination, an impression that does not go away. For others a specific word of Scripture leaps off the page. This happened to St. Augustine, who was converted by hearing children singing "Take it and read, take it and read." He took this as the voice of God telling him to open the Bible and read. When he did this, his Bible fell open to a particular passage that led to a complete redirection of his life. "As I came to the end of the sentence, it was as though the light of confidence flooded into my heart and all the darkness of doubt was dispelled."[20] On this point Tournier offers a telling reflection:

> I believe that God has a plan for every man [sic] at every moment. . . . I am quite certain that God reigns, that he rules the world, not only in general, but down to the tiniest details. He leads us men [sic] also, to the extent that we allow ourselves to be led, since he has granted us free-will. He does not only lead believers, but also unbelievers. It is the privilege of us believers to know it, and to be able to ask him in our prayers to lead us, and to listen in silence to his inspiration. . . . What is [God] asking him to undertake? That is what must be discovered; the natural thing is to go and ask him.[21]

The subtitle of this book is "Finding Your Calling for the Rest of Your Life." But to be honest, you cannot do it! Discerning your calling is a lifelong process. Maybe you thought you had it all figured out when you were twenty, or thirty, or forty. But in fact this delightful duty goes on and on and on. And it is especially important to re-engage this duty at important transitions in your life, such as retiring from remunerated work at fifty-five or sixty-five, or leaving your "second career" at seventy and facing "the third third of life." In fact, your calling remains about the same throughout your life, but the *expression of it* changes. There is only one once-for-all vocational decision, and that is to yield to the gracious invitation of God in Christ and to welcome being caught up in his grand purpose. Within that purpose, life is full of adjustments, decisions, redirections, mistakes, and even second chances.

---

20. Quoted in Peter Brown, *Augustine of Hippo: A Biography* (Berkeley and Los Angeles: University of California Press, 1967/2000), p. 101.

21. Tournier, *Learn to Grow Old*, p. 155.

The Discipline of Vocational Integrity

In his classic treatise on callings, the Puritan William Perkins says we must both enter and continue in our callings in a worthy manner. Vocational life is littered with idols — and not just during the most active and aggressive years of career development. In these years we encounter the idols of gain (being in it for the money), glory (seeking position for human approval), and instant ecstasy (getting a "fix" or a "high" from making a sale). All too easily a challenging profession or an all-consuming role like mothering can feed our addictions and become idolatrous. "Idolatry" is defined simply as making something one's ultimate concern other than the One who is ultimate. But even in retirement there are idols of self-gratification, pleasure, and seeking significance. Perkins reminds us that "walking worthy of one's calling" (Eph. 4:1) requires an ongoing process of sanctification of the worker and the work. He uses seventeenth-century examples of how not to walk worthily, examples that apply equally to today: for physicians, it is prescribing remedies without proper diagnosis; for booksellers, it is selling immodest and improper books; for the merchant and tradesman, it is having false weights and dressing up the wares so people are deceived; for the patron, it is, making a public pledge of a large gift but following through with only part of it; and for the landlord, it is jacking up the rents.[22]

Perkins continues by noting that the chief cause of a vocational mismatch is not being in the wrong location but yielding to the lust of the spirit. The lust of the spirit is the desire for something other than what God deems best for us. If we do not judge that the particular calling in which God has placed us is the best of all callings for us, we will yield to discontentment, as did Absalom, the sons of Zebedee, and Cain.[23]

To counteract this pernicious lust, Perkins offers several prac-

22. William Perkins, "A Treatise on Callings," *The Workes of That Famous Minister of Christ in the University of Cambridge, Mr. William Perkins* (London: John Legatt, 1626), p. 171.

23. Perkins, "A Treatise on Callings," p. 756.

tical measures: (1) discerning the initiative of God in our lives so that even in times of crosses and calamities we may rest certain that God has placed us in this calling;[24] (2) repenting if necessary for the wrong reasons we entered a calling (be it marriage, career, or ministry) but refusing to forsake our place and so continuing with diligence and good conscience — a strategy that is crucial for those who feel they entered marriage for the wrong reasons.[25] Further, Perkins advises (3) seeking sanctification of both the worker and the work by the Word of God and prayer;[26] (4) resisting the temptation to covetousness by laboring to see our particular situation as a providence of God, no matter how difficult it may be, and by resolving in our hearts that God — not a perfect situation — is our portion (Ps. 16:6); (5) turning our affections from this world to better things by not seeking more in this world than we actually need and setting our mind on heaven (Eph. 1:18);[27] and (6) persisting in our calling by pruning our lives of ambition, envy of others placed in "better" callings, and impatience, all of which incline us to leave our calling when trouble comes. On this last point, Perkins uses a medical image from the days before anesthesia that is superbly graphic. He says we must continue in our callings like the surgeon who continues to cut his patient even though the patient is screaming a lot![28]

Behind the deep spirituality of calling outlined by Perkins is an important truth: We are accountable on the last day for what we have done with our lives. The supreme motivating factor in walking worthy of one's calling is the fact that we must all give account on the day of judgment for what we have done in our callings. Perkins asks, "How then can we give a good account of ourselves before God on that day? We must calculate our blessings, weigh all that was defective, and then cleave to the surety of Christ, his death being all the satisfaction God needs."[29] This strongly biblical note (Matt. 25:19) is conspicuously missing in most Christian treatments

24. Perkins, "A Treatise on Callings," p. 760.
25. Perkins, "A Treatise on Callings," p. 762.
26. Perkins, "A Treatise on Callings," p. 766.
27. Perkins, "A Treatise on Callings," p. 770.
28. Perkins, "A Treatise on Callings," p. 773.
29. Perkins, "A Treatise on Callings," p. 779.

of vocational guidance. But what is particularly enlightening is to explore late-life purposes as experienced by the people of the Book, both in very ancient times and in the first century. This we will do in the next chapter.

Personal or Group Study: Bearing Fruit in Old Age: Psalm 92

Personal Reflection:
Reflect on when you were younger. Who among the older people in your life had an impact on you, taught you, or contributed to your growth? What were they like? What did they do?

Group Discussion:
Returning to the opening story of Frank and Nathaniel, how would you help each of them discern the next step of their lives, finding their calling for the rest of their days on earth? What questions would you ask them? How would you direct them to the dimensions of belonging and being as part of their calling? How could you help them explore how they are made, what brings them joy and has a sense of "I was born for this," and what serves others?

Read Psalm 92
1. The psalmist says it is good to praise the Lord (vv. 1-5). What are the benefits he sees in worshipping God? How many of these have you experienced in your own worship?
2. While the psalmist speaks of music and the ten-stringed lyre, he is obviously not limiting "morning and evening" to worship in the temple service as some Christians might limit worship to Sunday church services. How have you discovered worship in the context of everyday life?
3. In contrast, what does the psalmist see as the fate of those who are "fools" or "enemies" of God (vv. 6-11)? Do you agree that there is a direct relationship between acknowledging the greatness and goodness of God and long life? Why or why not?
4. As the author looks over his life, for what is he grateful (vv. 10-11)? As you look over your life, for what are you grateful?

5. What images does the psalmist use to describe old age (vv. 12-15)? How do these differ from the images presented by our own culture today?

6. What do you think is required for aging people to "bear fruit in old age"?

7. What do you think is required for people to "stay fresh and green"? Why do you think the psalmist ends this reflection with one more statement about the goodness of God?

8. How can you imagine yourself contributing to the next generation within the realities of your life now? What will you need to do to make this happen?

"To know how to grow old is the master-work of wisdom, and one of the most difficult chapters in the great art of living."

Henri Amiel, 1874[30]

30. Quoted in George E. Vaillant, *Aging Well* (New York: Little, Brown, 2002), p. 3.

3

Late-Life Calling and the People of God

*The elderly, as members of the ecclesial community, remain
called to a vocation, a ministry, to concrete practices of care.*

M. Therese Lysaught[1]

*If the task of young adults is to create biological heirs, the task
of old age is to create social heirs.*

George Vaillant[2]

In the modern Western world aging is a problem. In contrast, the
Eastern world, at least in the past, has regarded aging as a privilege
and has honored old people. At seventy-eight, I am considered, by
and large, somewhat obsolete. My title, "professor emeritus," has that
meaning: "honorably discharged from service." But when I go to
Asia, I am not "discharged from service." So there are great cultural
differences in how people approach aging. Even in the Bible there
are differences, many of which we will explore, but we do so recognizing that, with some significant exceptions, the expected span of

---

1. M. Therese Lysaught, "Memory, Funerals, and the Communion of Saints,"
in Stanley Hauerwas et al., eds., *Growing Old in Christ* (Grand Rapids: Eerdmans,
2003), p. 292.

2. George E. Vaillant, *Aging Well* (New York: Little, Brown, 2002), p. 144.

life was much shorter then than ours is today. Throughout much of biblical times the expected life span was about forty. So in this chapter we will first consider what the Bible actually says about the process of growing older. Then, exploring the narratives of the Bible, we will consider older people in the Bible and, insofar as we can ascertain, what it meant to them and to their society. Finally we will draw some conclusions.

Older People in the Old Testament — Pronouncing Judgment at the City Gate

In a brilliant study of what the Old Testament says about being human, Hans Walter Wolff shows how, along with the decreasing of powers, senses, and manifestations of life associated with aging, there are the honor and discerning role of the aged. "The older generation has to pronounce judgment at the gates of the city."[3] "The men with beards form the juridical assembly, something which king Rehoboam should have done instead of taking the advice of the young men."[4] Gray hair, notes Proverbs 16:31, is the crown of honor. But, Wolff says, age is not always wise.[5] Or, as someone once said, the one thing you cannot guarantee with old age is wisdom. Indeed, Scripture overthrows the biological rule that the older will rule the younger. God's choice is often with the younger: Jacob the younger rather than Esau the older; Joseph, the youngest son in the Jacob family; Samuel instead of the aging Eli; David rather than Saul; and, in the death scene for Jacob, the younger Ephraim rather than the firstborn Manasseh. The young man Elihu, in the Job narrative, respectfully waits to hear the flailing speeches of the older friends but raises the claim to be heard by the elder teachers of wisdom (Job 32:6-10).

Remarkably, in the Rule of St. Benedict, the abbot is called to

---

3. Deut. 21:2-6, 19f.; 22:15-18; 25:7-9; Ruth 4:2, 4, 9; Jer. 26:17.

4. Hans Walter Wolff, *Anthropology of the Old Testament* (Philadelphia: Fortress Press, 1974), p. 124.

5. Wolff, *Anthropology*, pp. 125-26.

listen to the youngest member of the community, who indeed may have wisdom from God. While generally older people are to be treated as wise elders, the Spirit of God can not only give wisdom and leadership to young people but may even reverse the normal process of aging, renewing youthfulness in the aging person. "Even youths grow tired and weary . . . but those who hope in the Lord will renew their strength." Such people will soar, run, and walk, "and not faint" (Isa. 40:29-31). Remarkably we see this happening especially in the New Testament.

Older People in the New Testament — from Seniors to Elders

The first mention of Jesus as "Lord" is made by an aging woman, Elizabeth, when she is visited by her cousin Mary, now a virgin pregnant with the Christ child. Elizabeth, further along in her pregnancy than Mary, experiences a quickening and says, "Why am I so favored, that the mother of *my Lord* should come to me" (Luke 1:43, italics mine). Then when Jesus is born and taken to the temple for dedication, it is two old people who see what is really going on, not the young graduates of the local Jewish yeshiva, or seminary.

Simeon was a righteous man "waiting for the consolation of Israel" when he experienced a revelation through the Holy Spirit that he would not die before he had seen the Messiah, God's anointed deliverer. The text says, additionally, that he was "moved by the Spirit" to go into the temple courts where he met the young holy family and the baby Jesus. Here is an old man sensitive to the Spirit's leading. Taking Jesus into his arms, he prophesied, "Sovereign Lord, as you have promised, you may now dismiss your servant in peace. For my eyes have seen your salvation." But the visitation of God's anointed was seen by Simeon not only for Israel, because Jesus would also be a "revelation to the Gentiles" (Luke 2:26-27, 29-32). Here is an old saint who envisages the global expansion of the kingdom of God to which Paul would later dedicate himself completely. He goes on to speak a prophecy to Mary and Joseph anticipating the complicated and divisive nature of the child's calling, and the impact of that calling on his parents. Is there something about a long obedience in the same direction that makes one especially open to the revelation of God in senior years? But Simeon was not the only elderly person to see what was going on.

Anna, an eighty-four-year-old godly widow, had devoted herself to fasting, prayer, and worship in the temple, as the text reads, "night and day." She came up to Mary, Joseph, and the child and "gave thanks to God and spoke about the child to all who were looking forward to the redemption of Israel" (Luke 2:38). If, in the Gospels, Elizabeth was the first confessor of the lordship of Christ and Simeon was the first to see the global reach of Christ's kingdom, Anna was the first evangelist, since she shared the good news about Jesus with others. Indeed, the only young people sensitive to what God was doing in these early chapters of Luke are Mary and Joseph and a band of motley shepherds who came from their fields because of an angelic visitation and went to see the child for themselves and then spread the good news.

Even the disciple Peter, through the actual words of Jesus (John 21:18), would survive to an age when he would be carried about and someone else would dress him. But he was faithful to the end. John, the so-called beloved disciple, after his incarceration on the island of Patmos for some years, spends, according to church tradition, his most senior years in Ephesus. And the apostle Paul, writing to the slave owner Philemon, declares that he is now an "old man" (Philem. 9) but is still pursuing the kingdom of God, travelling and nudging the infant Christian communities onward a notch. He says in a kind of epitaph, "I have fought the good fight, I have finished the race, I have kept the faith. Now there is in store for me the crown of righteousness, which the Lord, the righteous Judge, will award to me on that day — and not only to me, but also to all who have longed for his appearing" (2 Tim. 4:7-8). So, generally in the New Testament, old age does not mean reduced spirituality and diminished sensitivity to the Spirit of God. This is especially true when one considers the terms used in the New Testament for leadership in the people of God.

There is a rich diversity of words in the New Testament for church leaders, including of course overseers, deacons, and elders, but they communicate not so much the role or job description as they do the qualities of wisdom and character which older people have and which fit them to be mentors and leaders of younger people. Richard and Judith Hays note that "this usage presupposes that leadership is linked to seniority in the community."[6] They show that usually the words used for older people in the church do not communicate mere physical age, as with the word *palaios* (ancient), but rather leadership based on wisdom and character. "Unfortunately, because the single English word 'old' is used to translate this term as well as the word 'families' linked to *presbytes* (elder) and *geron* (old person), the pejorative connotations of *palaios* can bleed over and cause English readers to assign inappropriate negative associations to the other terms."[7]

So the New Testament does not primarily present older people as moving into spiritual decline. Just the reverse. As Richard and Judith Hays put it, "Nowhere are elders described as pitiable, irrelevant, behind the curve, as inactive and unproductive."[8] Whatever their physical limitations, they usually functioned as elders, mentors, counselors, and teachers. They were to be honored and cared for. This is especially evident in the teaching of Jesus about abandoning responsibility for parents (Mark 7:9-13), the warning of Paul (1 Tim. 5:8), and the exhortation of James (James 1:27). The prophecy of Joel foretold the outpouring of the Spirit on the Day of Pentecost, namely, that "your old men shall dream dreams" (Acts 2:17; Joel 2:28). This seems to be anticipated in the Psalms, especially Psalm 92:12-15.

Older People in the Psalms and Wisdom Books — from Obsolescence to Fruitfulness

The authors of the psalms, David and others, were realists. They were forthright in stating that aging is a period of physical decline.

---

6. Richard Hays and Judith Hays, "The Christian Practice of Growing Old," in Hauerwas, *Growing Old in Christ*, p. 5.

7. Hays and Hays, "The Christian Practice of Growing Old," p. 5.

8. Hays and Hays, "The Christian Practice of Growing Old," p. 11.

"All our days pass under your wrath; we finish our years with a moan. Our days may come to seventy years, or eighty, if our strength endures; yet the best of them are but trouble and sorrow, for they quickly pass, and we fly away" (Ps. 90:9-10). This is expanded by the professor in Ecclesiastes 12:1-8, who expounds the difficulties of old age using poetic metaphors to describe diminished mobility, sight, chewing ability, hearing, and taste: "The grinders [teeth] cease because they are few, and those looking through the window grow dim" (v. 3). Yet, as the psalmist affirms, our future is ordained by God. "All the days ordained for me were written in your book before one of them came to be" (Ps. 139:16). So how do they respond to this recognition that life in this world is limited, normally progressively so? There is an answer in the Psalms. "Show me, LORD, my life's end and the number of my days" (39:4). "Teach us to number our days, that we may gain a heart of wisdom" (90:12).

Wisdom is practical know-how for everyday living. The wisdom we can gain from numbering our days is recognizing the brevity of life and seeing the strategic importance of every day, living fully in the temporal and eternal at the same time. Bianchi notes that this is more than the mere mathematical calculation of the possible years ahead. "The numbering of our days . . . implies a pondering of the time ahead in its personal and social perplexities, as well as its promise."[9] The Jewish theologian, one of my favorites, sees this "numbering" as the sanctifying of time. "He who lives with a sense for the presence knows that to get older does not mean losing time but rather gaining time. . . . All it takes to sanctify time is God, a soul, and a moment. And the three are always there."[10] But there is more in the Psalms that illuminates the experience of aging.

The psalmists appeal to God for continuing divine support and blessing. "Do not cast me away when I am old; do not forsake me when my strength is gone" (71:9). And the reason they pray for continuing presence and blessing of God is to be able to "declare your

9. Eugene C. Bianchi, *Aging as a Spiritual Journey* (Eugene, Ore.: Wipf and Stock, 2011), p. 131.
10. Quoted in Bianchi, *Aging as a Spiritual Journey*, p. 164.

power to the next generation" (71:18). But it is Psalm 92 that best expresses the special gift of years.

> The righteous will flourish like a palm tree,
> They will grow like a cedar of Lebanon:
> Planted in the house of the LORD,
> They will flourish in the courts of our God.
> They will still bear fruit in old age,
> They will stay fresh and green,
> Proclaiming, "The LORD is upright;
> He is my Rock, and there is no wickedness in him. (92:12-15)

Generativity is one of the special marks of older people gaining wisdom. "They will still bear fruit in old age, they will stay fresh and green." Generativity is about investing in the next generation, mentoring younger people, being creative in work whether voluntary or remunerated, being a blessing to society and the church, being explorers and adventurers. As they conclude their study of aging in the Bible, the Hayses say, "In late life, Christians remain subject, to the possibility that God will act decisively in history and in their lives in such a way as to turn their lives upside down. They may be called to a new ministry. They may receive new revelation. They may see a long-awaited hope."[11] This openness to new discoveries, new adventures, and life-changing fruitfulness seems manifestly to be the experience of the aged characters in the Old Testament, certainly Moses, Joshua, and Samuel, but especially the people we know best — the patriarchs.

Older People in Old Testament Narratives

Abraham and Sarah — Aging in Faith but Not Seeing the Results
Abraham and Sarah, esteemed patriarch and matriarch, are really quite old when they receive life-changing revelations from God. But God came to them freshly. God promising. God making a cov-

---

11. Hays and Hays, "The Christian Practice of Growing Old," p. 17.

enant that God would personally belong to Abraham and Sarah. God committing to raise through this couple a large people of God, to invest in the land, and to be a blessing to all the nations. It was the "third third of their lives." This raises the question of the age of the patriarchs, something Derek Kidner comments on insightfully. Sarah, ten years younger than Abraham, is 65 (Gen. 17:17) and still enticingly beautiful. Abraham, to save his own life — fearing that down in Egypt they would kill him to get his beautiful wife (since she would then be a widow and marriageable) — gets Sarah to lie that she is his sister. As Kidner notes, "she seems an inordinately young sixty-five."[12] At Isaac's "miracle" birth Sarah is 90. Abraham is older in his up-and-down journey of faith, sometimes reaching amazing heights of trust in God, as when he prayed for Sodom and paid his tithe to Melchizedek, and sometimes falling back, twice to pass off his beautiful wife as his sister just to save his own skin. But he carries on, believing the promise given to him in Genesis 15:6 until he dies at 175. Sarah dies at 127.

Kidner notes that these life spans seem to be double our own, and this may well be, as noted in Deuteronomy 34:7, a special providence:

> Their continued vigor shows that this is no mere postponement of death but a spreading-out of the whole life process: e.g. Abraham at, say 110 in chapter 22 has the vitality of a man of, at most, seventy. Sarai's sixties would therefore presumably correspond with our thirties or forties, and her ninety years at Isaac's birth with perhaps our late fifties.[13]

Each of these faced faith issues in aging. For Abraham it was whether he could trust that God would do as he promised — provide a family, give him the land, and make him a blessing to the nations — even though he could not see this actually happening with a wife past childbearing age. Indeed, when the barren Sarah

---

12. Derek Kidner, *Genesis: The Tyndale Old Testament Commentaries* (Downers Grove, IL: InterVarsity Press, 1967), p. 117.

13. Kidner, *Genesis*, p. 117.

miraculously gave birth to a blood heir, Abraham had to take God at his word, believing as he and his son Isaac ascended the mountain for a sacrifice that God would somehow see that the family continued. This is reflected in the pithy and prophetic word to his servants as he takes Isaac up for the sacrifice: "We will worship and then *we* will come back to you" (Gen. 22:5, italics mine). For Abraham the issue was faith in God's ability to fulfill his pledge *even though he could not see the end of it all.* This is why in the famous chapter in Hebrews on the heroes of faith, Abraham is described as one "looking forward to the city with foundations, whose architect and builder is God. . . . All these people were still living by faith when they died. They did not receive the things promised; they only saw them and welcomed them from a distance" (Heb. 11:10, 13).

The passage in Hebrews ends with a beautiful word: "Therefore God is not ashamed to be called their God, for he has prepared a city for them" (11:16). We will all die without seeing the full result of that to which we have given ourselves in this life. This is part of the aging process. For Sarah there was a similar but different challenge.

Sarah was childless. And even though three mysterious visitors came to their tent-home, immortalized in the Holy Trinity icon of Rublev, a meeting in which she laughed at the thought that her wizened womb would bear a child, Sarah had to believe God could do the impossible. She got to see her own son, Isaac, but like many of us with families, she lived long enough to see how complicated the outworking of the development of the family is. Isaac marries Rebekah, who is childless. When Rebekah does have twins, Esau and Jacob, there is rivalry, jealousy, favoritism, and even murder threats within the family of promise. And Sarah dies without seeing the final reconciliation and *shalom* of the family when Jacob's children are reconciled with Joseph in Egypt. But that final scene with Jacob blessing his grandchildren in Egypt is highly evocative.

Jacob — Doing Death Work
Jacob's final passage gives us a window on the ministry of dying and death work.[14] Jacob had now lived in Egypt for seventeen years.

14. One of the deepest reflections of Richard and Judith Hays in their study

But as his death approached, he desired not only to provide for his burial by making Joseph swear with his hands cupped on his father's testicles[15] that he would not be buried in Egypt, but also that he would be carried to the land promised to his father, his grandfather, and himself (Gen. 47:28-31). Then Jacob worshipped as he leaned on his staff, thanking God for his grace and care through his life. His faith reached out to God in gratitude, the fundamental spiritual discipline. David, in his old age, similarly worshipped in dying (1 Kings 1:47-48).

Now Jacob must turn to the question of succession. Who will carry on the family of promise, will do the work of the kingdom and represent God's interests on earth? As Jacob's time draws near through illness, Joseph brings his two sons, half-Egyptian, half-Hebrew, to their grandfather for a blessing. Jacob has lost much of his vision, but when he hears that his son Joseph is present he rallies his strength and sits up in bed. He reiterates the promise that God made when he appeared to Jacob. There are two scenes in the final act.

First, there is an unexpected adoption. Apparently before Jacob realizes that his grandsons Ephraim and Manasseh are present, Jacob tells Joseph that he intends to adopt them into the family of promise, which is all the more extraordinary since they were born of an Egyptian mother. They "will be reckoned as mine . . . just as Reuben and Simeon are mine" (Gen. 48:5). In other words, they will not simply be grandchildren but, along with the other eleven sons, full bearers of the promise and of equal standing with Joseph himself. Joseph could never have anticipated this move on his father's part. They are then placed on Jacob's knees, which is the position

---

of Scripture is their musing on the fact of Jesus dying as a young man: "In old age as in youth, Christians are to take the Lord Jesus Christ as their model for their daily lives and interaction with others." Hays and Hays, "The Christian Practice of Growing Old," pp. 17-18.

15. Bruce Waltke notes that "put your hand under my thigh" is a euphemism for genitalia (Gen. 46:26; Exod. 1:5; Judg. 8:30). "When facing death, the patriarchs secure their last will by an oath at the source of life (see Gen. 47:29). The reason for this gesture is uncertain, but perhaps it is chosen because the oath involves the certainty of the posterity God promises." Bruce K. Waltke, *Genesis: A Commentary* (Grand Rapids: Zondervan, 2001), p. 327.

used for official adoption in the ancient world. This being done, Joseph removes them from Jacob's knees and bows his face to the ground. Then something deeply symbolic, laden with good news and saturated with grace, takes place.

Joseph brings them to their grandfather (now their father by adoption), in the manner one would normally expect, the older (Manasseh) placed next to Jacob's right hand, this being the place of preeminence and the rightful position for the firstborn, and the younger (Ephraim) placed by Jacob's left hand. But then Jacob does something that was wrung out of his lifelong theological education. Jacob crosses his hands, placing the right hand of priority on the younger boy and the left hand on the older. With his crossed hands he blesses both sons, praying that the angel who had delivered him from all harm might bless these boys, that they might be called by his name as well as that of Isaac and Abraham, and that they might flourish.

When Joseph notices that Jacob has placed his right hand on Ephraim's head, he becomes upset and tries to wrestle Jacob's dying hand away to put it on the head of the firstborn, Manasseh. Jacob says, "I know." What does Jacob now know? Jacob, himself almost blind, knows and deliberately follows God's unconventional plan. Jacob knows that grace does not follow natural preeminence, natural gifts, position in family, and human prominence.[16] Jacob knows the gospel, and his crossed hands symbolize what, under the new covenant with Jesus, came to be expressed as "at just the right time, when we were still powerless, Christ died for the ungodly" (Rom. 5:6).

Now a second scene takes place. With hands crossed, Jacob remembers Rachel. The memory of course was stimulated by the sight of Rachel's first child, Joseph, and Rachel's grandsons. She had never seen them because she had died in childbirth in the prime of life. But there is more to this than one more memory of his preference for Rachel over Leah, and the painful pleasure of remembering his late, most beloved wife. Jacob says: "As I was returning from Paddan, to my sorrow Rachel died in the land of Canaan while we were still on the way, a little distance from Ephrath. So I buried her there beside the road to Ephrath" (that is, Bethlehem) (Gen. 48:7).

16. This wonderful phrase comes from the theologian Karl Barth.

This is no mere death notice. It is spiritual death work. Here is the background. When Laban, Jacob's father-in-law, pursued Jacob with the hostile intent of searching for his household gods and his runaway daughters, Jacob swore that whoever had the *teraphim* (household idol) would die. We the readers know what Jacob does not know, that the *teraphim* are hidden under Rachel's saddlebag, upon which she is sitting. She had stolen them. When Laban enters her tent to search for them, Rachel complains that she cannot rise because she is having her period. However, years later when they are on the pilgrimage to Bethel, Jacob wants to clear the camp of idols. Gordon Tucker helps us capture the moment. "Imagine the heart-stopping, life-changing effect it must have had on Jacob. . . . Jacob discovers what we, the readers, have known all along: that he had unwittingly doomed his adored Rachel."[17] The next thing we hear is that Rachel has died in childbirth (Gen. 35:19). Was his oath her death sentence? Jacob's sorrow may have been doubly numbing.

First, there is something deep in the male psyche, that a man's seed planted in his beloved should cause such pain in childbirth, and in this case even death. Then added to this, but in an even deeper way, was the thought that Jacob had vowed her death unwittingly by his solemn word. Did he carry this burden through the rest of his life? And does this help explain his neurotic attachment to Joseph and Benjamin, children born to Rachel, and not to the children born to Leah? It seems that the blatant favoritism cannot fully be explained by the premature death of the mother of the boys. But what can Jacob do? By adopting Ephraim and Manasseh he can provide Rachel with more sons that she was denied having because of her untimely and premature death. But he was doing more.

His statement "to my sorrow Rachel died in the land of Canaan while we were still on the way" (Gen. 48:7) seems out of place in the adoption ceremony unless Jacob was doing something for his own soul in the lingering guilt he felt about her death.[18] We are

17. Gordon Tucker, "Jacob's Terrible Burden: In the Shadow of the Text," *Bible Review* (June 1994): 25-26.

18. Tucker argues that the Hebrew of "to my sorrow" can be translated "to die on account of." Thus Gen. 48:7 could be rendered: "When I was returning from Paddan, Rachel died on my account while I was still journeying in the land of Ca-

witnessing death work. He was dealing finally and fully, if not enigmatically, with his own feelings of Rachel's untimely death, a death that he had unwittingly willed. And in doing so, in this discipline of death, Jacob brought rest to his soul. It is in this context that Jacob says, "I know."

He knows that the love of God is revealed in all the passages of life — through the tears of a mother, through the strained relationships of a family, through reconciliations, through provision, through work, through childless love, and loveless fertility, through an untimely death, through pilgrimage on the way, through the surprise of seeing even your children's children. He knows that God's love is gratuitous.

Death concentrates life into a focused receptivity to God. On the one hand, it spells the end of all the achievement and performance one can accomplish in this life. On the other hand, it points beyond, to what will last and what is ultimately important. For David it was the provision of a successor.[19] For Jacob it was a memorial to the grace of God and a means of seeing the promise continued.

So What Do We Learn from These Older Saints in Both Old and New Testaments?

First, none of them abandoned their calling in their old age. Like them, we may retire from remunerated work but not from our callings. Second, old age did not solve outstanding personal flaws in their lives but usually exaggerated them. Third, the people we

---

naan, when still some distance short of Ephrath." Tucker argues that Jacob cannot die until he has unburdened himself of the guilt he feels over her death. "Great as his need is to confess, [Jacob] cannot simply say to Joseph on his death bed that he killed his mother. So he phrases his confession in a way that Joseph can well be expected to hear *metah 'alat* simply as 'died suddenly' or 'died to my sorrow,' while Jacob actually intends the same phrase to convey his confession, that Rachel 'died on my account.'" Tucker suggests that the "exquisite ambiguity allows Jacob both to shed his burden before Joseph, and probably to conceal it at the same time. Only in this way can we understand the enigmatic language of Genesis 48:7" (Tucker, "Jacob's Terrible Burden," p. 28).

19. "Praise be to the LORD, the God of Israel, who has allowed my eyes to see a successor on my throne today" (1 Kings 1:48).

studied were active in ministry in their senior years although obviously in an appropriate way given their health and physical stamina. Fourth, they received fresh revelation of God in their senior years. They remained open for newness in their relationship with God. They stayed "fresh and green."

Fifth, we see how some of them prepared to die. They did "death work" and died with a clear conscience inundated with the forgiveness and grace of God, and even forgiving themselves. Alex Miller in *Landscape of Farewell* proposes, "I have no doubt that we all harbour within us secret, dark histories of the soul, and that most of us take them to the grave with us, unreconciled and unshared. What consequences might arise for us, we wonder, from turning our imaginary histories into words?"[20] There is healing in such death work. These biblical people invested in the next generation and looked beyond the grave in hope. These discoveries point to the reality that aging itself is a spiritual journey, the subject to which we now turn.

Personal or Group Study: Luke 2:21-40; 1 Timothy 3:1-7

This personal and group study will focus on the ministry of aging people in the church. It applies of course to synagogues and other faith communities. As the gray tsunami affects the church, an aging congregation requires a lot of interest in ministry *to* seniors. It is generally agreed that older people have at least five needs: comfort, attachment, inclusion, occupation, and identity.[21] But in addition to ministry *to* seniors, we need to explore ministry *by* seniors. In biblical terms, this mean making a transition from regarding older people as seniors to regarding older people as elders. A Jewish book captures this in its title: *From Age-ing to Sage-ing.*[22] It is that subject to which we now turn.

---

20. Alex Miller, *Landscape of Farewell* (Crows Nest, NSW, Australia: Allen & Unwin, 2008), p. 120.

21. James M. Houston and Michael Parker, *A Vision for the Aging Church: Renewing Ministry for and by Seniors* (Downers Grove, IL: IVP Academic, 2011), pp. 197-99.

22. Zalman Schachter-Shalomi, *From Age-ing to Sage-ing: A Profound New Vision of Growing Older* (New York: Grand Central Publishing, 1995).

Personal Reflection:
Think of older people who have had an influence on your life. What was the context? Was it formal or informal? What has been the lasting value of their engagement with you?

Group Discussion:
Consider older people in your church fellowship. Are they mainly the object of ministry or the subject of ministry? Why is this so?

Read Luke 2:21-40
1. What preparation for ministry had been part of Simeon's life?
2. What makes him sensitive to the work of God in the situation when Mary and Joseph come to dedicate the baby Jesus?
3. What does Simeon do? What does Simeon say to God? What vision does Simeon have for the global impact of the church? What does Simeon say to the parents?
4. Simeon now feels he can be "dismissed in peace" (i.e., die). What would make you feel that your ministry on earth is complete and you could leave the future ministry to the next generation?
5. Each person's ministry is unique, so we cannot simply use Simeon as a model to copy, but what can we learn from Simeon's eldership that can be applicable in the contemporary church?
6. While Simeon's ministry was to the parents of Jesus, Anna's ministry was to the broader community. What does she say to people visiting the temple?
7. Anna's ministry and ministry preparation, like Simeon's, are unique (she was a widow who practically lived in the temple). But what can we learn from her life that would make her and us ready to minister at the right time?

Read 1 Timothy 3:1-7
8. The New Testament envisages the church being led by elders. What qualities does one need to function as an elder?
9. Since none of the qualifications for leadership listed are mere information or skills that can be learned at seminars or in a seminary, how might a lifetime of experience and service in the church be the best ministry preparation?

10. What can you do to move the church from concentrating on ministry *to* seniors toward ministry *by* seniors?

"A senior focused on work for the Lord is generally a happy, fulfilled and successful ager."

James Houston[23]

A Project in Church-Related Ministry — Intergenerational Storytelling

One of my doctoral students designed a wonderful way of connecting older and younger people in a church in mutual ministry. He designed a series of questions to be asked by younger people in the church of some of the older members, dredging out of the older people their stories of faith and service. In doing so the older believers actually mentored the younger ones. He paired people, sent the questions to them both in advance, and made sure each person had some kind of recording device. He suggested they take sixty to ninety minutes for the discussion. This storytelling approach could be used by others. Here are the questions he used.

- Where did your family come from and when did they arrive in this area?
- When did you first come to our church? How old were you and who invited you here?
- What were some of the memorable events in the life of our church in your early years here? When were the times you laughed, sensed God's presence, or felt like you were making an impact in the neighborhood?
- Describe the church building when you first attended. How has it changed?
- Were you baptized here?

23. Houston and Parker, *A Vision for the Aging Church*, p. 225.

- Have you or others you know made significant spiritual decisions through the ministries of this church?
- What positions have you held in this church? What church ministries/organizations have you been involved in?
- Why have you continued to remain in this fellowship, even through hard times?
- Why do you still follow Jesus?
- What do you consider to be significant events — good and bad — in the history of this church?
- How has the church changed or stayed the same during the years you have been here?

The pastor who did this project reported that "both young and old were pleased with the deeper connections they made with someone from another generation. One of the younger interviewers started a project of collecting the stories of challenges people have experienced and overcome."[24]

24. Matt Kitchener, "Stories of Our Life: An Intergenerational Storytelling Project with West Point Grey Baptist Church," for "Aging Matters" course (DMPM 949), Carey Theological College, Vancouver, BC, December 12, 2014.

PART TWO

Spirituality

....

4

Aging as a Spiritual Journey

Life is but one single way that leads to the kingdom of heaven.

Matthew the Poor[1]

Aging is more important as a spiritual than a biological process.

Eugene Bianchi[2]

Does aging automatically deepen our spirituality? Some would say the jury is out on this. George Vaillant, commenting on an extensive and longitudinal study, says that, in theory, aging should deepen our faith and spirituality because aging slows us down and teaches us to accept things we cannot change. And, of course, as we age we must contemplate death.[3] There is a saying that one's mind becomes very clear on the way to the guillotine. As you get older, there are plenty of signs that things are changing.

In *The View from Eighty*, Malcolm Cowley explains that you know you are old:

1. Matthew the Poor, *Orthodox Prayer Life: The Interior Way* (Crestwood, NY: St. Vladimir's Seminary Press, 2003), p. 164.
2. Eugene C. Bianchi, *Aging as a Spiritual Journey* (Eugene, OR: Wipf and Stock, 2011), p. 190.
3. George Vaillant, *Aging Well* (New York: Little, Brown, 2002), p. 278.

- When there are more and more little bottles in the medicine cabinet.
- When year by year your feet seem farther from your hands.
- When you fall asleep in the afternoon.
- When your bones ache.
- When you decide not to drive at night anymore.
- When, if you are wearing one brown and one black shoe, quite possibly there is a similar pair in the closet.[4]

My wife, now seventy-seven, struggles with diminished mobility as well as aches and pains. I run on 0.6 volts from my heart pacemaker and have episodes of Ménière's disease. This year I gave up skiing. I have trouble with my balance and had better stay off ladders. (Two of my friends had grievous falls, and one died from a fall from a ladder.) My wife and I have both lost some memory. But we are, I think, deeper. There are new questions and issues that arise through aging that demand answers with spiritual implications, but first we must ask what we mean by the word "spirituality," a notion that even professors of spiritual theology have difficulty defining.

Defining the Spiritual Journey

As a fool rushing in, I offer what I regard as the best definition of spirituality. It comes from a South American liberation theologian, Segundo Galilea:

> All spirituality springs from this fundamental fact of a God who loved us first. . . . If Christian spirituality is, before all else, an initiative by and a gift from God who loved us and seeks us, spirituality is then our recognition and response, with all that entails, to this love of God that desires to humanize and sanctify us. This path of spirituality is a process, concrete but never finished, by which we identify ourselves with God's plan for creation. Be-

4. Malcolm Cowley, *The View from Eighty* (New York: Viking Press, 1980), pp. 3, 4, 41, cited in Vaillant, *Aging Well*, p. 160.

cause this plan is essentially the Kingdom of God and its justice (holiness), spirituality is identification with the will of God for bringing this Kingdom to us and others.[5]

Briefly put, this means that spirituality is not about our attaining "human transcendence," something that is intrinsically oxymoronic, but spirituality is our responsiveness to the divine seeker in all of life. It is not attaining divine likeness by spiritual disciplines, making our way to heaven by spiritual effort. Simone Weil says it is like God crossing the infinity of time and space to knock on the door of our home, and he comes as a beggar. If we do not answer, like a beggar he keeps knocking. But then, Weil says, if we persist in not responding, the beggar goes away. Actually I do not think so. What happens is that our ears and hearts become so calloused that we no longer hear the knocking. If we respond, she said, he will come and have fellowship with us, and we must only not regret the marital *yes* we gave.[6] So the initiative is primarily from God, but we are not entirely passive.

The term "spiritual disciplines" is scary to many people. It suggests something hard, something to be endured. In reality it is recognizing that there are pathways to spiritual growth and to know God and God's purposes better. They are not attempts to move God-ward by our own sheer, dogged persistence and effort, pulling ourselves up by our own bootstraps. In fact, we cannot move an inch toward God by our own effort. The reality is that God crosses the infinity of time and space and knocks on our door. And that is precisely what spiritual disciplines do — they are ways of hearing the knocking and opening the door. They could more accurately be called disciplines of responsiveness to the seeking God. They act much as the friends of Lazarus did when Lazarus was dead in the tomb. The friends could not give life to their dead friend; only Jesus could do that. But the friends could move aside the stone so Jesus could speak the living word to the dead man.

---

5. Segundo Galilea, *The Way of Living Faith: A Spirituality of Liberation* (San Francisco: Harper and Row, 1988), p. 20.

6. Simone Weil, *Waiting on God: The Essence of Her Thought*, trans. Emma Craufurd (London: Collins, 1959), p. 91.

Perhaps the best definition of spiritual disciplines comes from the late Dallas Willard:

> A discipline for the spiritual life is, when the dust of history is blown away, nothing but an activity undertaken to bring us into more effective cooperation with Christ and his Kingdom. . . . Spiritual disciplines, "exercises unto godliness," are only activities undertaken to make us capable of receiving more of his life and power without harm to ourselves or others.[7]

Aging as a human experience should be an arena in which we become deeper spiritually, but it isn't that way for everyone. For some people, the process of aging is a spiritual wasteland, a backward movement, as they reminisce on the great days of youth and play themselves or consume themselves to the grave, or both. Part of the reason for this is the therapeutic culture that surrounds us like a fog.

The Trouble with the Therapeutic Culture

Keith Meador and Shaun Henson explain this therapeutic culture:

- Death can be avoided if we work hard enough and sufficiently trust our rational scientific abilities.
- The medical dream of having an average life expectancy of one hundred years is becoming a reality.
- Suffering and the contingencies of living and dying well are functionally denied.
- Health and youth are highly valued.[8]

Noting the research put into the longevity project, Meader and Henson summarize what some call the five medical categories under this

7. Dallas Willard, *The Spirit of the Disciplines: Understanding How God Changes Lives* (San Francisco: Harper and Row, 1988), p. 156.

8. Keith G. Meador and Shaun C. Henson, "Growing Old in a Therapeutic Culture," in Stanley Hauerwas et al., eds., *Growing Old in Christ* (Grand Rapids: Eerdmans, 2003), p. 90.

therapeutic culture: "the maintenance of perpetual youth, restoring of youth or rejuvenation, postponing of biological aging, prolonging of life, and finally the achievement of physical immortality."[9] They compare this with the Greek hero Tithonus, "who craved unending life and asked the gods for immortality. They granted his wish — but on achieving it he realized to his great horror that he had neglected to ask also for eternal youth. He simply grew older and more frail, in a never-ending nightmarish whirlpool of immortality."

Commenting on this, these authors say, "While attempting to feel good about ourselves by escaping death, we sometimes reach the point in our old age of fearing that it will never come soon enough."[10] So they conclude by contrasting the Christian world-view: "Growing old is not an enemy in the story Jesus gave us." Jesus calls us to take up our cross and follow him. By greedily clinging to "assiduously extended long lives in this world," we can lose hold of the words and life of Jesus, "while to give [our lives] up for Jesus, the gospel, the church, and others, is to retain them forever."[11] So, how is growing old not an enemy but a source of deepened spirituality? For many it starts not in late life but in the middle of life.

The Midlife Transition as a Spiritual Journey

We are simply asking different questions at different periods of our lives. In our forties we ask, What do I want to become? And in our fifties we ask, What difference am I making in my world? It is at this point that many, especially men who have devoted themselves to becoming successful in a career, try to find something signif-icant to do with the rest of their lives. They may view their "first half" and its accomplishment as empty and wonder whether their sacrificial involvement has really been significant. Have they made unworthy choices about their own development? Have they chosen their careers for ulterior motives? How have they hurt their imme-

---

9. Meador and Henson, "Growing Old," p. 95.
10. Meador and Henson, "Growing Old," p. 98.
11. Meador and Henson, "Growing Old," p. 110.

diate family and friends?[12] A hardworking property developer put it this way: "I have never made so much money and never been so unhappy." So how do people react to this?

Some are deniers. They refuse to accept that they are changing, that they are passing through a transition in which their questions, their aims, and their sense of satisfaction are changing. Others respond by a flight into lost youth. These are the ones who buy a fast car, abandon their wives or husbands of their youth and get a younger model, or take on extreme sports. "The middle-aged male attempts to defy time by proving his potency and desirability. He realizes that the sands are spilling quickly in the hour-glass of his life and believes that a new love affair will rejuvenate his vitality," says Bianchi.[13]

If hyperactivity is one response, hypoactivity is another. Many experience depression. They feel pressed down by the loss of their lives, their youth. And some reframe their lives after reevaluation and do something different. Some people at this point, if they are people of faith, want to go "into the ministry" feeling that they would be doing something of lasting value. Some, sadly, settle for a "second half" of life that is really a half-life. But all this may be avoiding the deeper questions that are surfacing, questions that prompt us to go deeper with God, ourselves, and others.

The questions we ask at transitional stages are spiritual dynamite. What is most important to me? (And do not quickly say, "God.") What values and virtues do I want to build my life around? What do I want to contribute to the world while I still have life? Whom do I love? What do I love? Can I, who have been so active, now go deeper with God in prayer and contemplation? In "The Stages of Life," Carl Jung said, "For a young person it is almost a sin, or at least a danger, to be too preoccupied with himself; but for the aging person it is a duty and a necessity to devote serious attention to himself."[14]

12. Bianchi, *Aging as a Spiritual Journey*, p. 17.

13. Bianchi, *Aging as a Spiritual Journey*, p. 31.

14. Quoted in Zalman Schachter-Shalomi, *From Age-ing to Sage-ing: A Profound New Vision of Growing Older* (New York: Grand Central Publishing, 1995), p. 85.

Midlife as a Spiritual Opportunity

Jung believed that every midlife transition is a spiritual crisis. "We are called to die to the old self (ego), the fruit of the first half of life, and liberate the new man or woman within us."[15] In "The Stages of Life," Jung wrote that "Wholly unprepared, they embark upon the second half of life."[16] He ponders whether there are schools that prepare people for this as there are colleges and schools that prepare people for the first half. Sadly, he concludes there are none. The afternoon of life cannot be lived according to the program of the morning.

> Instead of looking forward, one looks backward . . . one begins to take stock, to see how his life has developed up to this point. The real motivations are sought and the real discoveries are made. . . . But these insights do not come easily; they can be gained only through the severest shocks.[17]

Sue Monk Kidd comments on this as a gracious opportunity to go deeper.

> When the fullness of time comes, a sacred voice at the heart of us cries out, shaking the old foundation. It draws us into turbulence that forces us to confront our deepest issues. It's as if some inner, divine grace seeks our growth and becoming and will plunge us, if need be, into a cauldron that seethes with questions and voices we would just as soon not hear. One way or another, the

15. Quoted in Janice Brewi and Anne Brennan, *Mid-Life: Psychological and Spiritual Perspectives* (New York: Crossroad, 1982), p. 19

16. C. G. Jung, "Stages of Life," in *The Structure and Dynamics of the Psyche*, vol. 8 of *Collected Works of C. G. Jung*, trans. R. F. C. Hull (Princeton: Princeton University Press, 1960), p. 783, quoted in Sue Monk Kidd, *When the Heart Waits: Spiritual Direction for Life's Sacred Moments* (San Francisco: HarperSanFrancisco, 1990), p. 9.

17. Carl Jung, *Psychological Reflections*, ed. J. J. Jacobi (Princeton: Princeton University Press, 1971), pp. 137-38, quoted in Bianchi, *Aging as a Spiritual Journey*, p. 26.

false roles, identities, and illusions spill over the sides of life, and we're forced to stand in the chaos.[18]

But there are some misunderstandings about going deeper.

Some Caveats in Dealing with Midlife Transition

First, you do not have to go into the ministry or serve in a Christian parachurch organization to be doing "the Lord's work" or to be "doing ministry." We deal with this throughout the book, namely, that all good work advances the kingdom of God and so-called secular work is not less pleasing to God than religious work. What makes work holy is not the religious character of the work but the fact that it is done with faith, hope, and love. The dualism, that pernicious heresy that plagues the church worldwide, has been destroyed by Jesus. Dualism claims that religious work, such as pastoring, being a missionary, or engaging in social projects, has eternal significance and deep meaning while other kinds of work, teaching, crafts, trades, homemaking, and business, are innately secular and have no eternal significance.

Second, God does not have "a wonderful plan" just for the *second half* of your life — but a wonderful purpose for your whole life. Even the helpful book titled *Second Half* may affirm that unfortunate impression.

Third, God's calling for you is continuous, though the form it takes may change, and outlasts life in this world. So beware of abrupt changes.

Fourth, there are some differences between the way women and men experience midlife transition depending on their cultural background and whether, in the case of women, they have passed the childbearing years through menopause. Men, in contrast, do not have a dramatic physiological signal that they have moved into a new season in life.[19]

18. Kidd, *When the Heart Waits*, p. 10.
19. See Gail C. Stevens and R. Paul Stevens, "Menopause and the Male Climac-

If midlife becomes a spiritual opportunity, later life with its diminishing health and energy is a further spiritual opening and incentive.

Later Life Invitations to Go Deeper

The challenges in later life are similar to midlife but ramped up a notch. Aging people are challenged by the youth culture of society. Rapid changes, especially in technology and the Internet, leave aging people behind. Mobility and energy are reduced. Formalized and in-stitutionalized retirement sets people up for a season of continuous leisure and sloth. This leads to profound challenges to self-worth, as people are no longer identified by their career. In our industrial and information age, it is assumed that old age is a time of repose and disengagement, in contrast to older societies where older people were prized and engaged. Eugene Bianchi calls us not only to deal with these challenges on a personal level but also to discover their causes. "A spirituality for the aging calls for the courage of facing not only our own personal diminishments, but also the social network of oppression toward which we are both accomplices and opponents."[20]

Aging people experience progressive losses: parents, friends, colleagues, career, driver's license, and perfect health. Then life-threatening health challenges are encountered, usually heart disease or cancer. And finally, there is the certainty of death. There is a saying in French that when a person reaches midlife, the person knows the two railway tracks will converge on the horizon and he or she will die.

In these realities there are implicit spiritual incentives to grow. *First, experiencing intensification — toward a contemplative life.* This is the shift from essentially doing to being. Bianchi suggests that this period of life "offers one of the richest periods for growth

---

teric," in Robert Banks and R. Paul Stevens, eds., *The Complete Book of Everyday Christianity* (Downers Grove, IL: InterVarsity Press, 1997), pp. 624-29.

20. Bianchi, *Aging as a Spiritual Journey*, p. 152.

in meditative interiority."[21] Richard Rohr remarks on the shift that is taking place. "Basically, the first half of life is writing the text, and the second half is writing the commentary on that text. We all tend to move toward a happy and needed introversion as we get older. Such introversion is necessary to unpack all that life has given us and taken from us."[22]

At the extreme end of life in this world, my father, a very active and productive person through his youth and midlife, president of a steel company, had a double stroke at eighty years of age and spent his last years unable to speak and eat. He simply was. And I used to fly to Toronto, where he was hospitalized for much of the time, and sit by his bed, reading to him, praying with him, and perhaps most important of all, acknowledging that he was precious and a gift. Not that he *had* gifts or was using gifts but that *he was a gift*. Mom and Dad had a difficult marriage, but in those years my mother would do the same, as she was able. Daily she took the subway and bus to visit, often returning the pajamas she had taken home to wash. I often wished I could understand what my dad was thinking, feeling, and experiencing, but, alas, he could not speak. It is a sobering memory as I approach the age at which my mother died and my father became, for the first time in his life, quite ill. But on the way to that, which is the way we all go if we live into senior years, there is a transition from doing to being.

People used to say when I was the academic dean of Regent College, "Paul gets things done." I confess I used to hear this with a little pride. I am an energetic person, and when someone compliments me on this I often remind the person that I am also a serious sleeper, and so am fully alive and active during the day. But my energy is waning. I don't accomplish as much as I used to. So I too am into the process. I have more time for reflection, more awareness of who I am as a child of God, much loved not only by my wife, children, and grandchildren, but most importantly by God. This does not come from society but from aging.

21. Bianchi, *Aging as a Spiritual Journey*, p. 46.

22. Richard Rohr, *Falling Upward: A Spirituality for the Two Halves of Life* (San Francisco: Jossey-Bass, 2011), pp. 143-44.

Society presses us into the mold of accomplishments — CVs, accolades for things made and done, the places to which we have travelled, the jobs held, even roles we have undertaken in the church and not-for-profit organizations. But gradually we get asked less and less, like an international speaker who recently wrote me that "the invitations have dried up." For people whose life was wrapped up in their daily work, who lived for their work, actual retirement is a kind of death. And it is not surprising that some, mostly men, sometimes die shortly after retirement. There is nothing left to live for. But, short of physical death, this transition can be life giving if they shift to nurturing, discovering, and affirming who they are as a person, and especially a person in Christ.

New Testament authors use such a rich vocabulary to describe our being: priests, princes and prophets, new creations, sons and daughters of God, and companions in the kingdom of God (Rev. 1:9). These biblical descriptions are not individualistic identities but social ones, communal and people-of-God realities. And these "beings" are not something we have to accomplish. It is done. So Paul says, "So from now on we regard no one from a worldly point of view" (2 Cor. 5:16). This includes not looking at ourselves from a worldly point of view.

Bianchi explains both the challenge and the gift of moving toward a deepened spirituality. "Interiority, as a movement from outer-world to inner-world interests, is an ambitious notion in reference to the potentials of elderhood."[23] The surrounding culture presses us to realize our full potential, to express all our gifts, and to actualize ourselves. But this gets harder and harder to do as the years pass, even though there is a whole industry trying to help us recover our youth and experience everything that we can humanly appropriate. I am not saying that aging automatically cures us of self-centeredness, for that is manifestly not the case. Indeed, every twitch in our chest or new pain in our side can easily feed an obsession with ourselves — our health, our wealth, our welfare, and our possible demise. But there is at least an invitation in this process to deepen our spirituality, to seek a transcendent relationship with someone beyond our-

23. Bianchi, *Aging as a Spiritual Journey*, p. 191.

selves, to get to know God better, and to revel in the joy and delight of being sons and daughters of God (Rom. 8:15-17). Yes, there are deathbed conversions, and they are not to be despised. But more importantly, there is lifelong continuous conversion, as the Roman Catholics term it, on the way to death as we become more contemplative. Aging encourages this, but it also does something more.

Second, embracing simplification — toward a potent asceticism. Aging usually involves pruning our lives of some material things. The ancient philosopher Cicero, quoted in chapter 2, famously said, "Can anything be more absurd in the traveler than to increase his luggage as he nears his journey's end?" Yet this is what some people do. They build larger homes when they are empty-nested and accumulate more and more things. Most, however, reduce rather than increase things, and in doing so open themselves up to fewer encumbrances and fewer distractions.

Even today, Christian monks and nuns go into contemplative communities and some so-called spiritual athletes find a cave, or something like it, to attend to God without distraction. The distractions today are continuous music, the media, and ubiquitous advertising. While monks and nuns *choose* to do this culture-denying asceticism, our experience of aging with its attendant physical, emotional, and relational challenges invites us in the same way — to simplify our lives and to become contemplative. And it is not just a gentle invitation. Life persuades us, provokes us, pushes us, pulls us. Matthew the Poor is an Orthodox monk. He writes that "Life is but a single pathway to the kingdom of God."[24]

Recently I received an e-mail from a spiritual friend of almost half a century, Maurice Regnier, our French-speaking next-door neighbor in Montreal when we were first married. He put it this way:

> For me the outstanding feature in the last years has been the essential tendency towards greater simplification. Activities which energized me now leave me cold. I have no interest in acquiring literary, philosophical works as well as art books. Finally I am no longer tempted to buy discs. Far from me giving you the im-

---

24. Matthew the Poor, *Orthodox Prayer Life*, p. 164.

pression that I am now experiencing continuous boredom. It is just that certain things and activities which I liked in prior time sounds to me superfluous, without depth.[25]

Much is said in the Scriptures of the Old and New Testaments about a simpler lifestyle. The Israelites themselves are warned of the dangers of the too comfortable life of nice houses, growing herds, increasing income, and abundance of food (Deut. 8:11-19). Julie and Robert Banks reflect that

> Jesus' way of life exemplifies perfectly the simple, though not austere, way of life foretold of the suffering servant (Matt. 8:20), and his teaching encouraged an attitude toward possessions that was free of preoccupation and anxiety (Luke 12:22-32) and full of willingness to share them with those less fortunate (Luke 12:33-34). The early Christians in Jerusalem committed themselves to sharing some, though not all, of their resources with one another, especially with those in need (Acts 2:44-6; 4:32-5).[26]

They note that one of the best known sets of recommendations for dealing with goods and possessions was produced by the Central Committee of the Mennonite Church:

> Among its suggestions are recommendations for growing a vegetable garden as a family project, walking or cycling where possible instead of using a car, developing your own leisure activities alongside others that are available, using fewer disposables, lodging where feasible with friends when away from home, avoiding clothing fashions and fads, mending and reactivating old clothing instead of getting rid of it, buying used furniture, buying smaller cars, moving into a smaller house or sharing a house with someone, and refraining from shopping for recreation.[27]

---

25. Maurice Regnier, e-mail, December 16, 2013.

26. See Julie Banks and Robert Banks, "Simpler Lifestyle," in Banks and Stevens, *The Complete Book of Everyday Christianity*, pp. 896-900.

27. Banks and Banks, "Simpler Lifestyle," p. 899.

This points to a further implicit dimension of our spiritual journeys as aging people.

Third, cultivating practical heavenly-mindedness — living now in the light of the new heaven and new earth. One of the most common discussions today among aging people, following a famous movie, is what we have put on our "bucket list," that is, things we want to do, experience, and see before we die (or "kick the bucket," as the idiom puts it). Making a bucket list is usually triggered by a brush with a very serious disease that could be terminal. "What is on your bucket list?" Many people have a list: travel to Antarctica, see the Grand Canyon, do a bungee jump, spend a whole winter in Hawaii. There is nothing wrong with such a list except that it may reflect the need to squeeze out of this life everything we can as though there is nothing more. And there is more. A lot more. A wonderful more. And it is a "more" which the process of aging invites us to consider. For the Christian, the "more" is even better, more satisfying, and more lasting. Indeed, it is forever. It is the full experience of the kingdom of God and life in a new world with God's presence everywhere. Unfortunately, being "heavenly-minded" is so often equated with being no earthly good, being out of touch with reality now.

C. S. Lewis once wrote, "The Christians who did the most for the present world were just those who thought the most about the next. . . . It is since Christians have largely ceased to think of the other world that they have become so ineffective in this. Aim at heaven and you will get earth thrown in; aim at earth and you will get neither."[28] It is precisely this perspective that the last book of the Bible, Revelation, gives us: practical heavenly-mindedness.

The book of Revelation is not primarily a book of predictions. It is an exposé. It is how the world looks to a person in the Spirit. It is seeing life with bifocals, the present and the unseen spiritual world that will be fully manifested in the future. Unfortunately, this amazing book, full of images and dramatic actions, a kind of dissolve-fade slide show, has been the happy hunting ground for people who want to see a schedule of future political events. In reality, the

---

28. C. S. Lewis, *Mere Christianity* (London: Collins, 1952/1969), p. 116.

book is about reality, but reality in the light of God's ultimate future for planet earth and the people of God. The message of this book briefly is (1) God speaks to and dwells among his people. (2) God is in control; the Lamb, that beautiful image of Christ, is on the throne. (3) We are, however, facing a multidimensional opposition to righteousness in the world — systemic evil. (4) In the midst of our struggles God hears the prayers of people — in the first century this book was written to Christians in modern Turkey who were either persecuted by a hostile culture or seduced by a friendly culture. (5) In the meantime, the metaphor of the Christian life is martyrdom, laying down our lives. (6) There is a glorious future that is a presence (God is everywhere), a place (a new heaven and a new earth), and a people (God's people from every nation and people group). Who wants to go to heaven?

W. H. Auden said, "Nobody is ever *sent* to hell; he, or she, insists on going there."[29] Could the same be said of heaven? Far from being "pie in the sky by and by" or a hedonistic longing for pleasure, John's vision of God dwelling with his people is the consummation of faith. Creation is renewed. Evil is finally excluded. Jesus says about that future, "I am making everything new" (Rev. 21:5). The face of God is seen. Someone who would not want to be in God's presence would not want to go to heaven. But just how does all this enable us to live with *practical* heavenly-mindedness?

First, we will live with kingdom consciousness. We live and work in the certain hope of the final triumph of God's reign. But because the kingdom of God — right here partially and ultimately to come fully — is not just "spiritual," the line between "sacred" and "secular" is erased. All things are within the sphere of God's sovereignty and therefore God's concern. Ministry is much broader than church work. Concerns of social justice and evangelistic witness are necessarily held together.

Second, we will see time, more precious now than before, as a gift rather than just a resource to be managed. My friend Alec

---

29. W. H. Auden, introduction to *The Descent of the Dove: The History of the Holy Spirit in the Church*, by Charles Williams (New York: Meridian Books, 1956), p. viii.

writes me often about celebrating the temporary while holding on to the permanent.

> This Thursday morning, Dr. Nicely personally called me regarding the latest lab test finding. "Mr. Woodhull, I am amazed, surprised and delighted to tell you that we all were apparently wrong. I think Sir, somehow you again dodged a bullet! Your cancer is still very much there, but not of the virulent aggressive type that we all thought it was!" Sometimes news that your cancer is back is bizarre and strangely received as "good news"! My reaction is "I have bested this type of internal cancer before, and we think we can do so again!" Life is a struggle but with Him we can always handle the challenges and all kinds of troubles. Of course, I cannot totally relax, but I can rejoice as we again "celebrate the temporary whilst holding firmly to the permanent!!"! God is definitely being gentle with this his humble servant, and is yet so again![30]

"Everything today is for good purpose," says Alec at the beginning of another challenging day.

Third, we will invest in projects, work, and relationships that will last beyond the grave. This is a subject we will take up more fully later. But Scripture points to the truth that not just religious work, commonly called "soul" work, lasts, but all good work done with faith, hope, and love lasts. Elsewhere I have written extensively on how all good work in this world can be a participation in the kingdom, a partnering with God in doing "the Lord's work," contributing to a kingdom that will last forever.[31] This idea is easily misunderstood, and many a well-thumbed book about the "second half" of life describes retirement as a time when people want to shift from being successful to doing something significant. So, it is suggested by many, we contribute to the everlasting kingdom by getting into church work, doing short-term missions, teaching Sunday school, and aspiring to

30. E-mail, July 13, 2014.

31. See R. Paul Stevens, *Doing God's Business: Meaning and Motivation for the Marketplace* (Grand Rapids: Eerdmans, 2006); *The Other Six Days: Vocation, Work, and Ministry in Biblical Perspective* (Grand Rapids: Eerdmans, 1999); and *Work Matters: Lessons from Scripture* (Grand Rapids: Eerdmans, 2012).

be a church elder. While these are not bad things, they are not the only way we advance the kingdom of God in the divine-human conspiracy that is the coming of the kingdom. What matters is not the religious character of the work we do, whether remunerated or voluntary, but the fact that it is done with faith, hope, and love.

Paul has a pithy statement at the end of the resurrection chapter of 1 Corinthians, "Always give yourself fully to the work of the Lord [and he does not mean exclusively church work in this chapter], because you know that your labor in the Lord is not in vain" (1 Cor. 15:58). Ben Witherington III asks a pertinent question: "Are we creating and cultivating things that have a chance of furnishing the New Jerusalem?"[32]

Intensification, simplification, and practical heavenly-mindedness. Aging is a spiritual journey creating responsiveness to the seeking Father who loves us and wants to find us. Aging is not the progressive loss of humanity. Rather it is the reverse. Aging should make us more human and not less, and certainly more deeply human. Like all spiritual growth, we must cooperate with the God who loves us and seeks to humanize us. And this involves dealing with the vices of aging and nurturing the virtues of late life.

A Prayer by John Oxenham:

Lord, give me faith to live from day to day,
With tranquil heart to do my simple part,
And, with hand in Thine, just go Thy way.
Lord, give me faith! To trust, if not to know;
With quiet mind in all things Thee to find,
And childlike, go where Thou wouldst have me go.
Lord, give me faith! To leave it all with Thee.
The future is Thy gift, I would not lift
The veil Thy love has hung 'twixt it and me.[33]

---

32. Ben Witherington III, *Work: A Kingdom Perspective on Labor* (Grand Rapids: Eerdmans, 2011), p. 118.

33. Quoted in Dwight Hervey Small, *When Christians Retire: Finding New Purpose in Your Bonus Years* (Kansas City, MO: Beacon Hill Press, 2000), pp. 14-15.

Personal or Group Study: Living with Limitations:
Ecclesiastes 12:1-7; 2 Corinthians 4:7-18

Here is something no one wants to talk about. Aging involves progressive physical diminishment, not just the loss of perfect youthful health. There are other dimensions of struggle and loss — friends and family members predeceasing you; losing the identity and status of a career; reduced income; inability to engage in strenuous activities and sports; loss of youthful sexual virility; downsizing from the family house to an apartment, and then to a seniors residence; and the loss of a driver's license and complete independence.

The reality is that aging involves progressive relinquishment until we have only one treasure left — Christ and the relationships we have made through him. Through the process we discover that aging is a spiritual discipline. In this study we will marinate in an Old Testament reflection on aging and a more hopeful New Testament perspective.

Personal Reflection:
Name the things you have given up over the years. Which ones did you find most difficult? Did you feel the losses were forced on you against your will or did you voluntarily decide to give them up?

Group Discussion:
Share with the group your experience of finding new limitations in energy, work possibilities, travel, and mobility. What have you found helpful in coping with these?

Read Ecclesiastes 12:1-7
1. The author of Ecclesiastes takes a long hard look at life "under the sun," that is, without reference to a transcendent God, including the subject of aging. Unpack this elaborate metaphor of growing older, putting a name beside each of the figures of speech. Which ones deal with strictly physical losses and which ones are aesthetic, social, and spiritual?
2. With which losses can you identify, if any?
3. What conclusion does the author come to? In what way is his

conclusion different from saying "remember, you are going to die"?

4. Do you think it is easier or harder to seek and find God in old age?

Read 2 Corinthians 4:7-18

5. In Paul's second letter to the Corinthians, he lets us see inside a first-century Christian's world and experience. Here he reveals his own struggle with limitations. Name the kinds of challenges and sufferings Paul felt.

6. With which ones can you identify?

7. What hope does faith in Jesus bring to these difficulties? What is the basis of that hope?

8. It is sometimes said that one thing that is unique to Christianity is that it does not seek a supernatural escape from suffering but discovers a supernatural use for it. How could this be true for the limitations you face?

9. What have you learned from this study about living with limitations? In what way could you say that aging is a spiritual discipline?

5

The Vices of Aging

*A person's characteristics tend to become more accentuated
as his life goes on.*

Paul Tournier, psychiatrist[1]

*Methinks, our souls, in old age are more subject to trouble-
some maladies and imperfections than in youth.*

Michel de Montaigne (1575)[2]

Aging has its hazards. An early church father and pastor, Hermas,
writing to someone for whom he cared, made these observations:

Your spirit is now old and withered up and has lost its power in
consequence of your infirmities and doubts. For, like elderly men
who have no hope of renewing their strength, and expect nothing
but their last sleep, so you, weakened by worldly occupations,
have given yourself up to sloth, and have not cast your cares upon

1. Paul Tournier, *Learn to Grow Old*, trans. Edwin Hudson (Louisville: Westminster John Knox Press, 1991), p. 118.
2. Montaigne, quoted in Eugene C. Bianchi, *Aging as a Spiritual Journey* (Eugene, OR: Wipf and Stock, 2011), p. 134.

the Lord. Your spirit therefore is broken, and you have grown old in your sorrows.[3]

And in the late sixteenth century, Michel de Montaigne wrote similarly:

> We do not so much forsake vices as we change them, and, in my opinion, for worse. Besides foolish and feeble pride, an impertinent prating, forward and unsociable humors, superstition, and a ridiculous desire of riches when we have lost the use of them, I find there more envy, injustice, and malice. Age imprints more wrinkles in the mind than it does on the face; and souls are never, or even rarely seen, that in growing old do not smell sour and musty.[4]

It is not different for people today.

In this chapter we are reviewing some of these not-so-good character traits that may be evident in later life using a rubric which has a long tradition in the Christian church. For centuries this struggle has been understood through what are called the "seven deadly sins" (along with their Latin names): pride *(superbia)*, envy *(invidia)*, wrath *(ira)*, sloth *(acedia)*, avarice *(avaritia)*, gluttony *(gula)*, and lust *(luxuria)*. These "deadlies" have a long tradition in the Christian church. The earliest formulation came from the desert father and theologian Evagrius of Pontus (345-99). Evagrius and his followers went into the desert to be freed from the seductions of the world and to seek God wholeheartedly. What they found in the desert was that they had to deal with themselves, something aging people need to do and are often forced to do.

Gregory the Great, the sixth-century "Doctor of the Church" who finalized the list of seven deadly sins we know today, observed that these sins have generative capacity: they produce offspring. "From envy there springs hatred, whispering, detraction, exaltation at the misfortunes of a neighbor, and affliction at his

---

3. Hermas, quoted in Bianchi, *Aging as a Spiritual Journey*, p. 132.
4. Montaigne, quoted in Bianchi, *Aging as a Spiritual Journey*, p. 134.

prosperity," wrote Gregory. "From anger are produced strife, swelling of the mind, insults, clamor, indignation, blasphemies."[5] It is true, in a sense, that the seven deadlies are not actually sins but are *inclinations* to sin which, if left unchecked, will lead to sin and even crime. Anger, for example, can lead to murder. What is significant for the aging is that these inclinations can take a special form in the senior years of life. Age does not automatically produce sanctification! Or even wisdom. Indeed, aging may be like a magnifying glass pointing out what has been unchecked in earlier years. There is, however, another dimension to our exploration of the vices of old age.

Each area of struggle is a test inviting us to grow, to develop virtue (the subject of the next chapter). Our calling, as we have seen, includes living the lifestyle of God's covenant people.[6] But the vices are tests. Tests occurred all through Scripture, starting with Adam and Eve in the garden, who were faced with a test tree — the tree of the knowledge of good and evil. Even in the New Testament Jesus was led by the Holy Spirit into the wilderness to be tested (often the word is translated "tempted") by Satan. In each case there could be no growth in character and faith without a test. Take the opposite extreme of a parent who protects her child from every possible test and produces an immature adolescent who never grows up. No test, no growth. So, as we explore some of the special vices of old age, we can regard these as opportunities, as gateways to character growth. Take pride, for example.

Pride: All for Number One

In *Taking Your Soul to Work,* my colleague Alvin Ung and I develop the seven deadlies as they apply to work, the worker, and the workplace.[7] Here we are applying them to the aging process. Pride,

---

5. Quoted in William H. Willimon, *Sinning Like a Christian: A New Look at the Seven Deadly Sins* (Nashville: Abingdon Press, 2005), p. 21.

6. Significantly values have no opposites. But virtues have opposites — vices.

7. R. Paul Stevens and Alvin Ung, *Taking Your Soul to Work: Overcoming the*

we note, is attempting to appear above others, feeling conspicuous about oneself, being haughty and puffed up by self-conceit. Pride devises schemes to toy with the weak (Ps. 10:2). Pride causes us to deceive ourselves (Obad. 3). Does pride get reduced with the passing of time? John Cassian says: "For all other vices, as we said above, are sometimes diminished by the lapse of time, and disappear: to this one length of life, unless it is supported by skilful diligent and prudent discretion, is no hindrance, but actually supplies it with new fuel for vanity."[8]

One form of pride in the older person is the refusal to learn and the refusal to take instruction. As mentioned before, St. Benedict, in his famous instructions to abbots of his monasteries, enjoined that an older abbot must always listen to the youngest members of the community, who indeed may have wisdom. As aging persons, we find it all too easy to be self-centered as we recite our ailments and disabilities on the one hand, and boast of our life achievements on the other. In the literature of the ancient church, old people were described as garrulous. "The old are habitually talkative," says Macrobius in his *Saturnalia*.[9] The sayings of the desert fathers contain this confession: "When first we used to meet each other in the assembly and talk of what was helpful to our souls, we became ever more withdrawn from the things of sense, and mounted to the heavenly places. But now we meet, and spend our time in gossip and each drags the other downwards."[10]

Pride has a companion.

Nine Deadly Sins of the Workplace (Grand Rapids: Eerdmans, 2010), pp. 15-20. Some of the definitions of the "deadlies" were first published here.

8. John Cassian, *Institutes* 11.8 (*NPNF*, 2nd ser., 11:277), quoted in Rowan A. Greer, "Special Gift and Special Burden: Views of Old Age in the Early Church," in Stanley Hauerwas et al., eds., *Growing Old in Christ* (Grand Rapids: Eerdmans, 2003), p. 33.

9. Macrobius, *Saturnalia* 7.2.14, quoted in Hauerwas, *Growing Old in Christ*, p. 33.

10. *The Sayings of the Fathers* 105, in *Western Asceticism*, ed. Owen Chadwick, Library of Christian Classics, vol. 12 (Philadelphia: Westminster, 1958), p. 129, quoted in Greer, "Special Gift and Special Burden," p. 33.

Envy: The Pain of Seeing Someone Else's Good

Envy (*individa* in Latin) is a primal sin among the seven deadly sins.[11] Along with pride, envy was considered by the ancient doctors of the soul as the most intractable and pernicious of the seven deadlies, more so than lust or anger. Envy fuses together jealousy and selfish ambition. It is described as demonic (James 3:16). It is a magnet for other vices. It compounds the effects of other deadly sins. Envy is diabolical, said St. Augustine of Hippo, because we rejoice when we see the misfortune of a neighbor and feel displeasure when we see someone prosper.[12]

Paradoxically enough, the more we grow in virtue, the more susceptible we are to envy. So, even after Peter was forgiven and commissioned by Jesus thrice to feed his sheep (John 21), Peter couldn't help being curious about whether the Lord was treating a fellow disciple more favorably. "What about John?" Peter quizzed Jesus. But Jesus replied curtly that it was none of Peter's business.

It is easy to see how an aging person can experience envy of another's near-perfect health, near-perfect family (and what family does not have problems, though some seem to be blighted with catastrophic misfortunes?), or amazing financial resources to enjoy retirement while he or she ekes out a frugal existence until death. In an earlier chapter we noted how William Perkins regarded this as the *lust of the spirit* — wishing you had someone else's calling and not being content with your own. Paul speaks to this in the fourth chapter of Philippians when he remarks that he has learned the secret of being content, whether well fed or hungry, whether in plenty or in want. The secret, revealed in the same chapter, is to pray with thanksgiving, bombarding discontent with gratitude. However, many aging people store up a brooding anger.

---

11. Stevens and Ung, *Taking Your Soul to Work*, pp. 50-55.
12. Elaine Jarvik, "Envy — Sin That's 'No Fun at All' Has Elements of Pride, Greed, Anger," *Deseret News;* http://www.deseretnews.com/article/1,5143,635197503,00.html (accessed August 1, 2008).

Wrath: The Burning Desire to Control

Paul Tournier describes two kinds of old people.

> There are wonderful old people, kind, sociable, radiant with peace. Troubles and difficulties only seem to make them grow still further in serenity. They make no claims, and it is a pleasure to see them and help them. They are grateful, even astonished, that things are done for them, and that they are still loved. They read, they improve their minds, they go for quiet walks, they are interested in everything, and are prepared to listen to anyone. And then there are awful old people, selfish, demanding, domineering, bitter. They are always grumbling and criticizing everybody. If you go and see them, they upbraid you for not having come sooner; they misjudge your best intentions, and the conversation becomes a painful conflict.[13]

Behind the behavior of such a wizened old person, the second kind of person above, is an angry heart. In the Bible, anger is described as a burning, seething force that can be aroused in human beings and also in God. Two Greek words are used in the New Testament for our English word "anger." One *(orge)* means "passion, energy"; the other *(thumos)* means "agitated, boiling." Biblically, anger is God-given energy intended to help us solve problems. Not all anger is sinful and destructive. Examples of biblical uses of anger include Paul confronting Peter because of his wrong example (Gal. 2:11-14), David being upset over hearing Nathan the prophet sharing an injustice (2 Sam. 12), and Jesus getting angry over how some Jews had defiled the Gentiles' place of worship at God's temple in Jerusalem (John 2:13-18).[14]

Paul implies that not all anger is sin when he writes, "In your anger do not sin" (Eph. 4:26). The spiritual fathers of the church observe that anger has great force to fight against demons or destroy evil thoughts. Though anger is present in God in the form

13. Tournier, *Learn to Grow Old*, p. 118.
14. Stevens and Ung, *Taking Your Soul to Work*, pp. 38-43.

89

of righteous anger, and harnessed by Jesus Christ as zeal for God's house, most forms of anger residing within us are destructive. Anger turns to sin when it is selfishly motivated (James 1:20), or when anger is allowed to linger (Eph. 4:26-27). Instead of using the energy generated by anger to attack the problem at hand, one attacks the person instead. The next vice appears to be the exact opposite, not passion and energy turned the wrong direction, but passion and energy turned off!

Sloth: When the Very Thought of Labor Is Troublesome

The book of Proverbs inveighs against the sluggard and praises hard work. But there are more nuances to the matter than what appears at first sight. Here, it is assumed that even the slothful person works. The heart of the problem lies in the fact that the morally and spiritually lazy person is someone who prefers to whittle away at lesser problems while refusing to attend to the most important work at hand. The slothful person's appetite is never filled (Prov. 13:4). To be more exact, he actually has a huge desire to do what is righteous, but he simply refuses to spring into action to do what he knows he must do (Prov. 21:25-26).[15]

The Puritan Richard Baxter was eloquent in his description of sloth. He said the slothful person has an aversion to work, culls out of any assignment the easy part and leaves the hard part unattended to, is distracted by the slightest diversion. The slothful person does not care, has no heart, is almost dead. But how does the person who has quit work, or left a demanding career, experience sloth?

For many people retirement is unorganized sloth. It could be argued that of all the seven deadlies, sloth is the one most present with the aging. They have no initiative, no passion, no deep interest to explore, no concern to continue to make a difference. So they become couch potatoes in front of the television or, if they have the money, amuse themselves to death with one pleasure after another.

---

15. Stevens and Ung, *Taking Your Soul to Work*, pp. 44-49.

For our fiftieth wedding anniversary, my wife and I returned to the continent where we had spent ten meaningful years — Africa. We took the P&O boat from Cape Town, South Africa, up the west coast of Africa to Southampton, England. I spent much of the trip reading Lauren van der Post's *On Being Someone Other*, one of my favorite books, describing this trip in reverse. But on board we met a fascinating couple. They, ninety-five and ninety-three years of age, respectively, were not actually married. As he said, "Why would I marry this lovely widow and have her lose her pension!" But this was their twenty-seventh cruise. They literally would get off one boat and on to the next — very expensive sloth not within the reach of some people. But the sloth that is within reach of most aging people leads to boredom. Many people are literally bored to death.

Sloth is not just a time-management problem requiring more scheduling. It is a soul condition. Abba Moses, according to John Cassian, said the old "pass their old age in lukewarmness and in sloth, and so obtain authority not from the ripeness of their character but simply from the number of their years."[16] And its solution is a soul remedy, being recaptured with a magnificent obsession, our beautiful God and his coming kingdom for which we passionately pray every day, "Your kingdom come, your will be done on earth as it is in heaven" (Matt. 6:10).

Avarice-Greed: The Desire for More

People usually regard greed as the drive to achieve and acquire more, in the shortest time possible. Ironically, this passion makes us feel discontented with what we have and obsessed with what we do not yet have. The fourth-century Christian monk Evagrius of Pontus, who spent the final decade of his life in prayer and scrutiny of his unruly emotions, wrote that greed is not merely the tendency to accumulate more material things. Greedy people, said Evagrius,

16. John Cassian, *Conferences* 2.13 (*NPNF*, 2nd ser., 11:314), in Greer, "Special Gift and Special Burden," p. 33.

are preoccupied with "thinking about what does not yet exist."[17] The Ten Commandments calls this variant of addictive thinking "covetousness."[18]

Biblically, greed or avarice (Latin word: *avaritia*) is generated when our desire for God is channelled toward the things that God has made. At the root of it is the inclination to regard bread (or provision) as something distinctly separate from God. We see this dynamic at play within the heart of humanity, in the garden of Eden, where Adam and Eve found themselves gazing at the fruit from a tree. The fruit was good for food (provision), it was a delight to the eyes (beauty), and it would make them wise (power), they mused. In the garden of plenty, they were tempted with provision, beauty, and power. They faced an ageless conundrum that confronts us today: Would they turn to God and trust him to provide for their needs (in want or in plenty)? Or would they satisfy those desires in whatever means seemed fit to them? Alexander Schmemann, a prominent twentieth-century Orthodox Christian priest and writer, observed that Adam's primal sin was much more than munching on a forbidden fruit. "The sin is that he ceased to be hungry for Him and for Him alone, ceased to see his whole life depending on the whole world as a sacrament of communion with God."[19]

Greed is especially a temptation (and a test) in old age as we often, in the words of one wife, have, as previously quoted, "twice as much husband and half as much money." Can we trust God for provision? And if greed, as Evagrius said, is thinking about that which does not exist, aging people can be greedy for life, thinking about all they might have done, all they might have accomplished, and — here is the "bucket list" back again — all they must do and experience before they die. Meanwhile, there is always food.

---

17. Paul Jordan-Smith, "Seven (and More) Deadly Sins," *Parabola* 10 (Winter 1985): 41.

18. Stevens and Ung, *Taking Your Soul to Work*, pp. 21-25.

19. Alexander Schmemann, *For the Life of the World: Sacraments and Orthodoxy* (Crestwood, NY: St. Vladimir's Seminary Press, 1973), pp. 11, 18.

Gluttony: Living to Eat Rather than Eating to Live

We usually associate gluttons with grossly obese people and Roman bacchanalia or *vomitoria*. But we cannot judge gluttony by bodily appearances alone. Some obese people are "cursed" with glandular problems while other gluttonous people are "blessed" with a high metabolic rate — looking slim and trim even after stuffing their faces. Gluttony encompasses much more than guzzling supersized drinks. Eating disorders, such as anorexia, are arguably a reverse form of gluttony.

The sin of gluttony lies in finding satisfaction through excessive consumption. We use the word "gluttony" for a variety of excesses: "He is a glutton for work." "She is a glutton for punishment." "He's a glutton for attention." Gluttony is about having too much of a good thing, be it excessive television, sex, leisure, company, or work. Gluttony putrefies life-giving activities into addictive indulgence. Since medieval times, Christian thinkers and philosophers have linked lust and gluttony. Both indicate a lack of self-control (which, as we will see, serves as the Spirit's life-giving resource that enables us to live well).

In a narrower sense, gluttony is an inordinate preoccupation with food and eating. This often happens in aging persons as they move from eating to live to living to eat. On a basic level, gluttony reduces our energy for work and relationships. We become preoccupied with self-pleasure rather than caring for others. Ultimately, gluttony drives out mindfulness of God and people. The first test faced by Adam and Eve came through eating; their failure to obey resulted in alienation from God. This is tragic because God has always intended food, work, and fellowship to go together.

Pope Gregory I defined the vice of gluttony in five ways: "Sometimes it forestalls the hour of need; sometimes it seeks costly meats; sometimes it requires the food to be daintily cooked; sometimes it exceeds the measure of refreshment by taking too much; sometimes we sin by the very heat of an immoderate appetite."[20]

20. Gregory I, *Moralia* 30.18, quoted in Gerard Reed, *C. S. Lewis Explores Vice and Virtue* (Kansas City, MO: Beacon Hill Press, 2001), pp. 62-63.

That brings us to the last of the seven deadlies, the one many think is not a factor in aging.

Lust: That Inner Craving to Possess Another

Lust is commonly thought of as an intense sexual desire for someone else. The feelings are accompanied by a craving for gratification and excitement. From a Christian perspective, the word "lust" is commonly translated in Greek as *epithymia*, a sexual sin that perverts the God-given gift of sexuality. As with all the seven deadly sins, the early beginnings of this one occur as a thought, disposition, or attitude that eventually leads to action, including fornication, adultery, and other sexual perversions. Jesus said as much: "I tell you that anyone who looks at a woman lustfully has already committed adultery with her in his heart" (Matt. 5:28).[21]

Sexuality in itself is good. It involves physical, psychological, and spiritual dimensions of the human person created by God. The word "sex" (*secare* in Latin) connotes that something has been cut apart that longs to be reunited. Franciscan priest Richard Rohr notes that sexuality ensures that we would never miss the fact that we are hardwired for relationship: "It is so important that we know that we are incomplete, needy and essentially social that God had to create a life-force within us that would not be silenced."[22] Indeed, Rohr says it will not be silenced until ten minutes after we are dead! To that thought we will return.

Sexual arousal is normal, healthy, and good. But to allow that arousal to become a fantasy of a sexual affair with someone who is not your marriage partner means that arousal has become lust, the desire to possess another. This life force must therefore be directed. Protestant reformer Martin Luther famously said that it is one thing to have a bird land on your head — you can hardly stop the arousing thoughts from popping up in your head from time to time. But it is quite another to let the bird build a nest there.

21. Stevens and Ung, *Taking Your Soul to Work*, pp. 26-31.
22. Richard Rohr, "An Appetite for Wholeness," *Sojourners* (November 1982): 30.

The great saint and doctor of the church, Augustine of Hippo, wrote deeply and insightfully about the idolatrous appeal of lust in his autobiography *The Confessions*. He said lust disturbs the whole person, mingling mental and physical craving. "So intense is the pleasure that when it reaches its climax there is an almost total extinction of mental alertness; the intellectual sentries, as it were, are overwhelmed."[23] But do older people experience lust? Are they not sexually dead or on the way to being sexually dead? Not so. The desire for intimacy and affection, built into us by our Creator, does not die but continues throughout life. It is true that men peak in adolescence and gradually decline while women peak in their mid-thirties and tend to maintain that level throughout their lives.

Indeed, there are special temptations in this area that come with aging. It is often observed that old men get married; old women get lonesome. Often older men realize that while they have the desire (and are aroused), their virility, their capacity to engage in sexual intimacy in the complete sense of sexual intercourse, is waning. And so they abandon the wife of their youth, to quote Malachi (1:14), and take on a younger model. It seems Solomon became a specialist at this as he took on several hundred young and beautiful women to feed his lust. These new wives, most of them foreign beauties, led him astray from a single-minded devotion to God. So he ended badly. Unlike Solomon, how can we end well in this area of sexual attraction?

The critical spiritual discipline for aging people is acceptance. And one crucial area to be embraced is a normal reduction of sexual appetite and capacity for intercourse. This does not mean, however, that older people are desexualized and have no appetite. The reverse is true, especially in a long marriage: simpler forms of intimacy and affection can take on a deeper meaning. The reality, as someone put it, is "the lights may be on, but the voltage is low."

Sexuality in late life (when partners are available) is neither rare nor inappropriate. In general, sexual activity does decrease

---

23. Quoted in Stanford M. Lyman, *The Seven Deadly Sins and Evil* (Dix Hills, NY: General Hall, 1989), p. 55, italics mine.

with age, but there are major individual differences among the elderly. . . . Moreover, forms of physical intimacy should be distinguished from sexual intercourse: "The voltage is never too low for affectionate physical contact. Such contact may help keep the lights on."[24]

We will die as sexual beings and be resurrected into the new heaven and new earth, in some way beyond our imaginations, as fully human beings, more human than ever before, including our sexuality, though without the mortal this-worldly form of marriage, as Jesus said (Matt. 22:29-32).

Seven deadlies. Seven tests and seven challenges to grow. Each of them is an opportunity to appropriate from God, in a divine-human conspiracy, the fruit of the Spirit.[25] Virtues, as we will see, do not grow on trees to be easily picked, but are wrung out of life in the rough and tumble of living with ourselves and others, but doing so in the presence and resource of God. In this way aging people can become men and women of virtue and wisdom. As Rowan Greer says, "It is not merely long persistence in virtue that gives the old authority, it is also the fact that they have themselves struggled sometimes unsuccessfully, for the virtue that is the true basis of authority."[26]

Carlo Carretto lived silently among Muslims in North Africa as a witness to Christ. But, like the desert fathers and mothers before him, he had to encounter himself. In his *Letters from the Desert* he wrote about this:

In the depths lodges the most crucial fault, greater than any other even though it is hidden. It rarely, or perhaps never, breaks

---

24. J. W. Rowe and R. L. Kahn, *Successful Aging* (New York: Pantheon Books, 1998), pp. 28-30, quoted in James M. Houston and Michael Parker, *A Vision for the Aging Church: Renewing Ministry for and by Seniors* (Downers Grove, IL: IVP Academic, 2011), pp. 118-19. Read the excellent chapter on this subject by Patricia Jung, "Differences among the Elderly: Who Is on the Road to Bremen?" in Hauerwas, *Growing Old in Christ*, pp. 112-28.

25. In *Taking Your Soul to Work*, Alvin Ung and I link each deadly sin with one aspect of the Spirit's fruit.

26. Greer, "Special Gift and Special Burden," p. 30.

out in single concrete actions pushing towards the surface of the world. But from the depths, from the inmost layers of our being, it soaks in a poison which causes extreme damage. . . . Because it is hidden, or rather camouflaged, we can barely catch sight of it, and often only after a long time; but it is alive enough in our consciousness to be able to contaminate us and it weighs us down considerably more than the things we habitually confess. . . . They are hidden and general sins we cannot rid ourselves of: laziness and cowardice, a falsehood and vanity, from which not even prayer can be entirely free. . . . The time for playing games at spirituality, for "Let's pretend," is over. . . . There we can live but on alms, and on the grace that can neither be known nor grasped.[27]

Personal or Group Study: The Temptations of Age: Genesis 27:1-40

"A person's characteristics tend to become more accentuated as his life goes on," says Paul Tournier, noted Swiss physician.[28] These are often traits that were unaddressed in earlier life but become exaggerated in later life. In this study we are considering one biblical character, the patriarch Isaac, who in later life was vulnerable to a fault that was unaddressed in earlier life. Some commentators on the Genesis story remark that the high point in Isaac's spiritual life seems to have been in his youth when he voluntarily allowed himself to be bound by his father to be sacrificed. It seems downhill from then on. One of the reasons for this persistence of temptation is his unaddressed favoritism of one son, Esau (Gen. 25:28), and his sensuality expressed in his addiction to the taste of wild game. Behind it all is not only a sensuality but also a secularism in his refusal to obey the word from God given to Rebekah his wife, namely, that

27. Carlo Carretto, *Letters from the Desert* (Maryknoll, NY: Orbis Books, 1972/2002), pp. 61-62.
28. Tournier, *Learn to Grow Old*, p. 118.

"the older will serve the younger" (Gen. 25:23). We will open the study in a dramatic encounter.[29]

Personal Reflection:

Briefly review your own life in terms of the most persistent temptation from youth to the present. Has it increased or decreased?

Group Discussion:

Discuss the quotation by Paul Tournier above. Do you agree, or do you think this is an example of ageism, projecting on to the old the faults we see around us?

Read Genesis 27:1-40

1. The blessing of the next generation in the ancient Hebrew world involved two stages. First, there was the birthright by which the older would receive two-thirds of the inheritance (Deut. 21:15-17), something which Jacob, the younger, stole from his brother Esau. Second, there was the blessing by which normally the oldest would become the leader of the family tribe. Here old Isaac wants to bless Esau even though God had prophetically announced that the usual order should be reversed. What makes Isaac vulnerable at the time of blessing?

2. What do we learn about the marriage relationship of Isaac and Rebekah? What do we learn about the relationship of Esau and Jacob? What connection is there between these two realities?

3. When in your own life have you been vulnerable because of an unhealthy dimension of your family experience? How might this vulnerability be amplified in the aging process?

4. Isaac is obviously confused when faced with Jacob's deception. In his blindness, why does he identify Jacob by smell rather than by the sound of his son's voice?

5. When Isaac realizes he has blessed the wrong son, who is really

---

29. For a fuller account and the larger story of the family, see R. Paul Stevens, *Down-to-Earth Spirituality: Encountering God in the Ordinary, Boring Stuff of Life* (Downers Grove, IL: InterVarsity Press, 2003).

the right son, he cannot revoke the blessing. What does this tell us about the power of blessing?

6. When, if ever, have you been blessed by parents? When have you been able to bless the next generation?

7. One psychiatrist suggested that as Isaac hugged Jacob, thinking it was Esau, this was what Jacob had always wanted — his father's approval and affection. But then Jacob must have thought that his father believed he was showing his love for his brother! What hunger do you have in your own soul that has not been satisfied in your family upbringing? How do you see this playing out in your life?

8. What could Isaac have done in his earlier life to prevent this amplified temptation?

9. What can you do to deal with your own persistent temptation?

Now or Later:
Identify how each of the "seven deadlies" may appear in the life of older people you have known.

6

The Virtues of Late Life

Becoming elderly may require a significant retooling of the virtues one had prior to the change.

Charles Pinches[1]

"Lord God, you have called your servants to ventures of which we cannot see the ending, by paths as yet untrodden, through perils unknown. Give us faith to go out with good courage, not knowing where we go, but only that your hand is leading us and your love supporting us."

The Lutheran Liturgy of Evening Prayer[2]

This chapter is even more challenging than the chapter on vices, which we developed under the rubric of the seven deadly sins. It is easy to succumb to a vice. It is a lot harder to embrace a virtue. But we saw that the vices we experience can be agents of renewal and growth. Even some contemporary journals have highlighted the

---

1. Charles Pinches, "The Virtues of Aging," in Stanley Hauerwas et al., eds., *Growing Old in Christ* (Grand Rapids: Eerdmans, 2003), p. 204.
2. *Lutheran Book of Worship* (Minneapolis: Augsburg, 1978), p. 153, quoted in Gilbert Meilaender, *Should We Live Forever? The Ethical Issues of Aging* (Grand Rapids: Eerdmans, 2013), p. 102.

experience of, and sometimes even the educational opportunities afforded by, the vices.[3] But who advertises the virtues? And why not? Imaginary sin is attractive whereas real sin is not very pretty, and real goodness is actually beautiful but imagined goodness is not. Before we explore real good, virtues, an important distinction must be made, especially because so many people, businesses, organizations, and even churches advertise their values, not their virtues.

Values are cherished ways of behaving, but they have no opposites. You have your values and I have mine. But virtues are ingrained character traits and they have opposites — vices. In this chapter we are exploring some critical questions: Are there virtues that are distinctive to the aging person that are especially invited and evoked by the aging process? Further, do the classic virtues that we inherited from Greece and Rome and that were largely adopted by the Christian church need retooling for people who are aging? The Lutheran prayer cited above stresses the virtue of courage, one of the classical virtues from the ancient world. Aristotle identified twelve moral virtues and nine intellectual virtues, but traditionally Christian teaching has identified four cardinal (or hinge) virtues: prudence (wisdom), justice, temperance (self-control), and fortitude (courage). Next we must ask how the three distinctively Christian virtues of faith, hope, and love work out in the aging person? Finally, we need to ask, How do we get virtues?

Distinctive Virtues for the Aging

Author Charles Pinches compares the aging process to the aging of wine, about which we say things like "This wine is aged to perfection." But he is careful to compare the modern and postmodern perception of aging to the aging of a banana — not so much "aged to perfection" as "overripe." Not only are we bombarded with entreaties to avoid any signs of aging, as William May observes, "The aged thus

---

3. See "What Is the Deadliest Sin?" *Economist* (June 14-20, 2014): 6-9, and "The Seven Deadly Sins: Turn Temptations into a Source of Strength," *Scientific American Mind* (November/December 2013): 25-53.

slip to the margins of consciousness for the ruling generation . . . [as the aged] squander the resources of generations to come."[4] No, neither aged to perfection nor just overripe. And yet . . .

There are character traits that emerge and are evoked by the process of aging. From ancient times, continence is one of the virtues associated with old age. Gregory Nazianzus, from the early centuries of the church, asked the elderly why they delayed baptism until just before death (as many of them did). "Why do you fear youthful passions in deep old age and at your last breath?"[5] John Cassian, another early church father, "suggests that humility in the aged is a great virtue, since it represents the overcoming of pride and vainglory, vices that can be associated with old age."[6]

Further, it can be argued that as people adapt to a smaller and smaller range of activities and experience progressive diminishment, they develop patience. Gilbert Meilaender rightly notes that patience is not simply resignation but is "finding freedom within the necessities that constrain us."[7] These necessities include losses, diminished capacities, and the loss of life's giftedness. Apparently Arthur Rubinstein gave concerts at age eighty. When asked how he did it, he said that he played fewer pieces, played the slow movements more slowly so the fast movements would appear fast, and practiced the pieces more often.[8]

In the area of work, the late mentor of Pope John Paul II, Cardinal Wyszynski, notes that patience is the virtue evoked by our experience in the work world. "The prime virtue gained through daily work," says Wyszynski, "is patience. Here is a ladder, as it were, by which we go ever higher in our ordinary, daily work." The temptations against longanimity (faithfulness) are many: "the longing for new work, unfaithfulness in the work we have already undertaken or that has been entrusted to us, the desire for a change of occu-

---

4. Quoted in Pinches, "The Virtues of Aging," pp. 203-4.

5. Quoted in Rowan A. Greer, "Special Gift and Special Burden: Views of Old Age in the Early Church," in Hauerwas, *Growing Old in Christ*, p. 26.

6. Quoted in Greer, "Special Gift and Special Burden," p. 27.

7. Meilaender, *Should We Live Forever?* p. 33.

8. Paul B. Baltes, "Facing Our Limits: Human Dignity in the Very Old," *Daedalus* 135, no. 1 (Winter 2006): 35, quoted in Meilaender, *Should We Live Forever?* p. 84.

pation and this, sometimes, for some quite trivial reason. There is always a certain streak of betrayal in these feelings."[9] But the same could be said for the exigencies of aging, which underscore once again the deep truth of Matthew the Poor's statement that "Life is but one single pathway to the kingdom of God."[10] The earlier version of Wyszynski's book had the intriguing title *Working Our Way to Heaven*, but could it not also be said that we are aging our way to heaven? Meilaender argues for this: "Old age in particular . . . is a gift — a blessing that not only requires patience of us but, more significantly, offers the opportunity for patience."[11] William May, quoting *The Patient's Ordeal*, calls one indigenous virtue simplicity: "Simplicity should mark the elderly, and not merely because memory lapses into the familiar, repetitive grooves, but because the pilgrim has at long last learned to travel light. He has learned to live by simple truths and simple gifts."[12]

In one sense the three theological virtues — faith, hope, and love — encompass the classic virtues. Faith gives wisdom. Love gives justice and temperance. Hope gives courage. It is well known that the triad of faith, hope, and love appears multiple times in the Bible together, and singly throughout the New Testament.[13] We will consider them one by one.

The Theological Virtues

The virtue of faith is simply a hearty responsiveness to God. The Danish philosopher Søren Kierkegaard once compared the experience of faith to a person going into the ocean to swim but keeping his toe on the bottom as he moved out from the beach until that moment

9. Cardinal Wyszynski, *All You Who Labor: Work and the Sanctification of Daily Life* (Manchester, NH: Sophia Institute Press, 1995), pp. 123, 141.

10. Matthew the Poor, *Orthodox Prayer Life: The Interior Way* (Crestwood, NY: St. Vladimir's Seminary Press, 2003), p. 164.

11. Meilaender, *Should We Live Forever?* p. 86.

12. William May, *The Patient's Ordeal*, p. 134, quoted in Pinches, "The Virtues of Aging," p. 210.

13. See 1 Thess. 1:3; 1 Cor. 13:13, Col. 1:5.

when he abandoned himself to the buoyancy of the water. That is faith — abandoning oneself to the support, succor, and beauty of God. Does aging automatically generate more faith? Empirical observation does not support the view that people become more faith-full in age in spite of some quite spectacular deathbed conversions. Most turning to God seems to happen in adolescence, and some people wane in faith as they grow older. Others experience an expansion of faith to an increasing universalism — that all the religious paths lead to the same mountaintop. But one thing is for certain, old age requires faith, and might even evoke it.

As people age, they see many of the organizations they have served turning inward, abandoning their mission, or simply dying. Their churches seem to be dying, and their families have multiple problems, some insurmountable. To finish well with a sweetness toward God, with faith and trust, is a virtue desperately needed. An elderly New Mexican storyteller expressed this faith in an interview: "There are some joys to old age, but none greater than realizing that finally you are learning about the really important things. Perhaps God reveals some of His mysteries to us at the very end before He receives us."[14] But it does raise the issue of hope, the second of the Christian theological virtues.

The virtue of hope is believing that the whole human story is straining toward a beautiful end, the second coming of Christ, the full inauguration of the kingdom of God, bringing shalom, and the renewal of everything in a new heaven and new earth. As a generation, we are often without this hope. We do not see *through* the wars, famines, and plagues, through the breakdowns of families and of the social fabric of societies, to envision the world and its peoples going somewhere. How can investing in the next generation be worthwhile? It is sometimes said that of the three — faith, hope, and love — the one most needed today is hope. Edward Collins Vacek says, "More and more, one works for a future that others, not oneself, will enjoy."[15] In the

14. Eugene C. Bianchi, *Aging as a Spiritual Journey* (Eugene, OR: Wipf and Stock, 2011), p. 184.

15. Edward Collins Vacek, S.J., "Vices and Virtues of Old-Age Retirement," quoted in Meilaender, *Should We Live Forever?* p. 57.

New Testament, Simeon is an example of dying in hope (in contrast to hoping to die), which Charles Pinches expounds beautifully:

> Simeon's hope in the Messiah carries him to his death in the knowledge that the good life he has lived . . . is not futile precisely because it need not save itself. Put another way, it does not need to bring itself to its own completion. . . . The virtue of hope, in other words, makes possible the end of a life without the end of a story. In this sense Simeon has lived toward the coming of the one who will bear his story up into new life, the form of which Simeon has, in hope, caught only a glimpse. In this knowledge he can go peacefully to his own death.[16]

With Simeon we can go peacefully to our death knowing the best is yet to come even though we will not see it. The apostle Paul alludes to this in his sermon in Pisidian Antioch, sweeping through the history of God's people: "Now when David had served God's purpose in his own generation, he fell asleep" (Acts 13:36). We will not see the end, but we can serve God's purpose in our lifetime. This hope is often evoked by the fragility of our bodies.

The process of physical diminishment and the struggles we have in this "mortal tent," to quote the apostle Paul, are actually invitations to go deeper with God and to have hope. This involves transforming mortality and anticipating resurrection. In 2 Corinthians 4 the apostle Paul is writing his second or perhaps third letter to the struggling church in Corinth. If in 1 Corinthians we get to see inside a first-century church, in 2 Corinthians we see into the heart of a first-century Christian — the apostle himself. In this book Paul makes himself vulnerable about his own struggles, physical, emotional, relational, and vocational. But he argues that they are good for him and them, not in the sense of "feeling good" but in the true sense of being better and deeper.

> Even if our outer humanity is decaying, our inner humanity is being renewed day by day. This slight momentary trouble of ours

16. Pinches, "The Virtues of Aging," p. 222.

is working to produce a weight of glory, passing and surpassing everything, lasting forever; for we don't look at the things that can be seen, but at the things that can't be seen. After all, the things you can see are here today and gone tomorrow, but the things you can't see are everlasting. (4:16-18)[17]

N. T. Wright's exposition of this is so cogent and timely that I wish to quote it extensively:

It's easy to imagine, within the worldview that many have today, that . . . he's saying that bodily things, outward things, don't matter. . . . He is talking not about "physical" and "non-physical" things, but about the *present* world as contrasted with the *future* world. The point about "things you can see" is that they last for only a short while. But God's true reality, which will one day be brought to birth in his new world, is more richly physical in ways we can hardly imagine, though at present out of sight. All we know about it is that it will involve "a weight of glory." . . . Now Paul declares that the glory we presently have, which is like treasure in earthenware pots (verse 6), is as nothing compared with the glory that is yet to be revealed. And in that light even the huge, overwhelming, deadly sorrows and difficulties that Paul endured appeared as "slight momentary trouble." He had come to realize that the present body is only the beginning, the initial clothing for a true self that will one day be more fully clothed. That is totally different from saying "the present body is the outer shell for a true self which is non-bodily and will one day, thank God, be freed from the whole business of bodies." It is more like saying: "I live in a tent at present, but one day I shall live in a palace!"[18]

Hope enables us to invest in the next generation and in projects that will outlast our lifetime. It enables us with Simeon and David

---

17. I am using N. T. Wright's translation here: *Paul for Everyone: 2 Corinthians* (London: SPCK, 2003), p. 46.
18. Wright, *Paul for Everyone*, pp. 50-51.

to die in peace. It assures us that even our difficulties in this life, physical, emotional, and psychological, are in a way preparing us for a greater life. But if hope is needed for aging, so is love. *The virtue of love is caring loyalty to people, places, and communities.* Ironically, as we age we might become less a professional (in the usual sense of that word, especially as it applies to our work life) and more an amateur (in the true sense of that word). The root meaning of "amateur" is a person who works or serves for love, out of love, in love. This involves loving God (glorifying God in all), loving our neighbor for the common good, loving the world, caring for and unfolding the potential of creation as co-creators, and loving ourselves — not having a self-esteem based on comparisons and achievement but accepting God's value placed on us. Not surprisingly, the apostle Paul says that love is the greatest thing of all.

One thing does not cease with aging, even when physical energy is flagging and people face increasing medical challenges, and that is the command, which is also an invitation, to love our neighbor (Matt. 22:39). But for many people retirement, as Stuart Babbage says, "can degenerate into a life of appalling selfishness, narcissism and self-indulgence, but retirement can also make possible a life of loving thoughtfulness and service."[19] My wife, Gail, herself struggling with diminished mobility after three back surgeries, still visits people, especially people in seniors' residences and hospitals. She sends cards to people needing cheering up and finds ways of serving other faculty wives and faculty women at the University of British Columbia. Another person, Al, continues to use his practical skills to help widows and needy people with household improvements. Others cook meals and host street people in "Out of the Cold" programs that receive people off the street for a night's rest and a good meal in a church. Service clubs thrive on voluntary activity. Christians have been especially prominent in the creation of such institutions. An older book written by a Canadian is a superb answer to the critique that "the church has never

---

19. Stuart Barton Babbage, "Retirement," in Robert Banks and R. Paul Stevens, eds., *The Complete Book of Everyday Christianity* (Downers Grove, IL: InterVarsity Press, 1997), p. 859.

done the world any good." E. H. Oliver in *The Social Achievements of the Christian Church* chronicles the amazing service rendered by individual Christians and the church, usually as volunteers, from the first century to just before the Second World War.[20] And there is a lot of history since 1930 — including microeconomic development, volunteer service projects, Habitat for Humanity, short-term mission trips, and hospital auxiliaries, just to name a few. These endeavors were often staffed by seniors. Such practical, loving service is actually good for us. In their fine book on retirement, William and Judith Diehl quote an interesting financial newsletter (since many people say they cannot afford to give their service free of charge): "Generous people are rarely mentally ill. On the other hand, let us not be critical of our stingy friends. Remember, stinginess is an illness. Some don't dare give; they might run out. My dear friends, of course you are going to run out. You can't take it with you. The ill individual narrows his vision until he ceases to see the multiplicity of opportunities."[21]

So what does it mean to love our neighbors, and how do we do this as aging people? The Catholic theologian Thomas Aquinas outlined what he called the corporal (bodily) alms deeds and, alongside these, the spiritual alms deeds. They form a handy outline of all the ways we can love our neighbor. The corporal alms deeds are:

- To feed the hungry
- To give drink to the thirsty
- To clothe the naked
- To harbor the harborless
- To visit the sick
- To ransom the captive
- To bury the dead

The spiritual alms deeds are:

20. Edmund H. Oliver, *The Social Achievements of the Christian Church* (Vancouver: Regent College Publishing, 1930/2004).

21. From the Ministry of Money Newsletter, edited by Don McClanen (February 1997), quoted in William E. Diehl and Judith R. Diehl, *It Ain't Over Till It's Over: A User's Guide to the Second Half of Life* (Minneapolis: Augsburg Books, 2003), p. 134.

- To instruct the ignorant
- To counsel the doubtful
- To comfort the sorrowful
- To reprove the sinner
- To forgive injuries
- To bear with those who trouble and annoy us
- To pray for all[22]

Using Aquinas's outline, we can develop some ways that ministry can be undertaken *to* seniors in terms of both corporal (bodily) service and spiritual alms deeds. Elders often need transportation, in-home services and visitation, financial advising and financial assistance, safety, late-life planning, help to live with chronic conditions, and initiatives to facilitate aging in place (aging at home). The huge aging generation is a challenge for loving service.

James Houston and Michael Parker note that "caregiving will be the great test of character this century. . . . Almost half of those eighty-five or older, one of the fastest growing age groups, face the possibility of dementia (about two-thirds will be diagnosed with the dreaded Alzheimer's disease). Recipients of such a diagnosis are virtually guaranteed years of dependency on others."[23] They later describe the primitive church in the middle of the second century. The church in Rome was caring for 1,500 widows and, in a kind of sexual revolution in reverse (where Christian girls chose virginity rather than an early arranged marriage to an older man), the church looked after thousands of virgins. There were 3,000 virgins in the church of Antioch. Houston and Parker opine, "The aging of our society may demand radical changes, but never anything so remarkable as the sexual revolution in reverse of the early church."[24]

But, tragically, almost all seniors ministry is service *to* aging people, especially in churches. Houston and Parker continue:

---

22. Thomas Aquinas, "Treatise on Faith, Hope and Charity," *Summa Theologica*, part II of second part, qu. 32, art. 2.
23. James M. Houston and Michael Parker, *A Vision for the Aging Church: Renewing Ministry for and by Seniors* (Downers Grove, IL: IVP Academic, 2011), p. 39.
24. Houston and Parker, *A Vision for the Aging Church*, p. 100.

Our research confirms that "senior ministry," when present at all, is almost universally considered to be a ministry *to* rather than *from* elders. The reciprocity of exchange, in the vein of the great exchange we have from Christ, is absent. . . . The implication is that older persons have nothing to offer younger generations. . . . The ever-growing, aging church is no burden; instead this burgeoning reservoir of accumulated experience and talent can provide a lasting legacy of God's love to the younger generations.[25]

So we can use Aquinas's list as an outline of how aging people can contribute to others as they are able. In doing so seniors can become elders, those able to mentor and encourage the younger generation, comforting the sorrowful, counseling the doubtful, visiting the sick, and, above all, praying for others. Richard Rohr says about eldering, "First of all, you can only see and understand the earlier stages from the wider perspective of the later stages. This is why mature societies were meant to be led by elders, seniors, saints, and the 'initiated.' They alone are in a position to be true leaders in a society, or certainly any spiritual organization."[26] The Jewish rabbi Zalman Schachter-Shalomi calls this transition from "age-ing to sage-ing." "Spiritual eldering deals with developing contemplative skills, harvesting one's life, leaving a legacy for the future and preparing for death."[27] Rabbinic literature contains the following reflection: "He who learns from the young is like one who eats unripe grapes and drinks wine from the winepress. But he who learns from the old is like one who eats ripe grapes and drinks old wine."[28]

Yes, many of the roles of older people in simpler societies have been taken over by doctors, counselors, herbalists, psychiatrists, schoolteachers, professional politicians, and therapists. But there still is need for mentoring, and aging people can give something younger

---

25. Houston and Parker, *A Vision for the Aging Church*, p. 20.

26. Richard Rohr, *Falling Upward: A Spirituality for the Two Halves of Life* (San Francisco: Jossey-Bass, 2011), p. 9.

27. Zalman Schachter-Shalomi, *From Age-ing to Sage-ing: A Profound New Vision of Growing Older* (New York: Grand Central Publishing, 1995), p. 39.

28. *Abot* 4:20, quoted in Houston and Parker, *A Vision for the Aging Church*, p. 55.

people cannot give. Indeed, the need is desperate, and aging people can do it. This is part of the retooling of societies and communities like churches and synagogues that is needed. So the nurturing of virtues and the retooling of communities must go side by side.

Faith, hope, and love are core virtues that, as Charles Pinches said above, "may require a significant retooling of the virtues one had prior to the change." For example, faith is responsiveness to God, but at an age when we are no longer striving to succeed in a career, or when drivenness is reduced, we may deepen our resting in God as our portion, our bounty, and our delight. Martin Luther called this "confidence with God," and he used a profound analogy.

> When a husband and wife really love each other, have pleasure in each other, and thoroughly believe in their love, who teaches them how they are to behave one to another, what they are to do or not to do, say or not to say, what they are to think? Confidence alone teaches them all this, and even more than is necessary. For such a man there is no distinction in works. He does the great and the important as gladly as the small and the unimportant, and vice versa. Moreover, he does them all in a glad, peaceful, and confident heart, and is an absolute willing companion to the woman. But where there is any doubt, he searches within himself for the best thing to do; then a distinction of works arises by which he imagines he may win favour. And yet he goes about it with a heavy heart and great disinclination. He is like a prisoner, more than half in despair and often makes a fool of himself. Thus a Christian man who lives in this confidence toward God knows all things, can do all things, ventures everything that needs to be done, and does everything gladly and willingly, not that he may gain merits and good works, but because it is a pleasure for him to please God in doing these things. He simply serves God with no thought of reward, content that his service pleases God. On the other hand, he who is not at one with God, or is in a state of doubt, worries and starts looking for ways and means to do enough and to influence God with his many good works.[29]

29. Martin Luther, "Treatise on Good Works," in W. A. Lambert, trans., James

Such confidence comes from hope. In our younger and middle years, hope is invested in looking to the long-term success of our active-years ventures, but as we age we wish to see something even better — the full coming of the kingdom of God associated with the visible and bodily return of Jesus and the transformation of everything. Our love may well become more universalized. Paul Tournier speaks of a "passage to universal commitments." Eugene Bianchi, commenting on this, envisages "A search for new ways of human bonding, wider forms of love, commitment to the universal concerns of humankind. . . . [A person] becomes less a consumer and more a sharer of material and spiritual resources."[30]

Faith, hope, and love — the consummate character traits desirable in aging people. Are these virtues innate? Are they something we obtained by mind control, as the Greek philosophers claimed and as part of the church has maintained through its emphasis on "moral education"? Are virtues a sheer gift of God for which we have no part? Or is there a shared work of God and humankind?

Virtues Can Be Nurtured

True education, as Augustine noted, is to learn what to desire. Character is influenced by habits, and habits are formed by choices. So there is some possibility that moral training can help in the cultivation of virtues. But there is more to it than learning, knowing, hearing about, and even wanting these virtues. Biblical revelation offers something substantially different that appears to be "foolishness" from the perspective of Greek philosophy (1 Cor. 1:22-25). The gospel declares that God gives what he requires, that the grace of the new creation accomplishes what never can be obtained by reason

---

Atkinson, ed., *Luther's Works*, vol. 44 (Philadelphia: Fortress Press, 1966), pp. 26-27. Calvin said, "We have not an uncertain God of whom we have created a confused and indistinct apprehension but one of whom we have a true and solid knowledge" (*Comm. Ps.* 4:2). Salvation for Calvin was knowing God and knowing ourselves. This double knowing is the work of the Spirit, the *testimonium internum*, and internal persuasion (*Institutes* 3.2.14-16).

30. Bianchi, *Aging as a Spiritual Journey*, p. 210.

or moral effort alone. Virtues are not obtained solely by "pulling ourselves up by our own bootstraps." They are gifts of God.

But they are gifts that invite and even require human cooperation. That is surely what is behind New Testament exhortations to "think about such things" (Phil. 4:8) in the context of a list of commendable character qualities, "get rid of" vices like slandering (Eph. 4:31), "make every effort to add to your faith goodness" (2 Pet. 1:5), and "live a life of love" (Eph. 5:2). The virtuous life engages the whole person in what must be seen as active prayer. But it is not autonomous activity. Rather than simple human achievements, certainly not ones we might boast about having attained, virtuous living is essentially responsive and always God-centered. Faith, hope, and love keep us focused on the source — the God of all true virtue. Peter says that God's divine power "has given us everything we need for a godly life through our knowledge of him who called us by his own glory and goodness [aretē]" (2 Pet. 1:3). Paul reminds the Colossians that it is as "God's beloved" that they are to clothe themselves with goodness and patience (Col. 3:12). What Athens requires, Christ inspires.[31] It is the result of a divine-human conspiracy so that every time we cry for help, whether orally or existentially, God comes. This is summarized beautifully in a statement of the apostle Paul and applies to the virtues of aging: "Work out your salvation with fear and trembling, for it is God who works in you to will and to act in order to fulfill his good purpose" (Phil. 2:12-13). How these virtues become part of our legacy is something we will take up in the next section. This divine-human cooperation in nurturing virtues is reflected in the following prayer.

The Prayer of an Anonymous Abbess

Lord, thou knowest better than myself that I am growing older and will soon be old. Keep me from becoming too talkative, and

---

31. Much of this section on how we get virtues was first published by myself and Iain Benson in "Virtues," in Banks and Stevens, *The Complete Book of Everyday Christianity,* pp. 1069-72.

especially from the unfortunate habit of thinking that I must say something on every subject and at every opportunity.

Release me from the idea that I must straighten out other people's affairs. With my immense treasure of experience and wisdom, it seems a pity not to let everybody partake of it. But thou knowest, Lord, that in the end I will need a few friends.

Keep me from the recital of endless details; give me wings to get to the point.

Grant me the patience to listen to the complaints of others; help me to endure them with charity. But seal my lips on my own aches and pains — they increase with the increasing years and my inclination to recount them is also increasing.

I will not ask thee for improved memory, only for a little more humility and less self-assurance when my own memory doesn't agree with that of others. Teach me the glorious lesson that occasionally I may be wrong.

Keep me reasonably gentle. I do not have the ambition to become a saint — it is so hard to live with some of them — but a harsh old person is one of the devil's masterpieces.

Make me sympathetic without being sentimental, helpful but not bossy. Let me discover merits where I had not expected them, and talents in people whom I had not thought to possess any. And, Lord, give me the grace to tell them so. Amen.[32]

Personal or Group Study: Finishing Well: 1 Kings 10:14–11:13; 1 Samuel 12:1-5; 2 Timothy 4:6-8

Sometimes business and professional people become very successful and begin to amass fortunes, multiple houses, and multiple and very expensive luxury cars, and take fabulous and very expensive vacations, and their central love for Jesus and his kingdom grows cold. They may continue to show up for church services when they are not playing golf or travelling, but the passion for God has gone. They give in to consumerism, to having the latest, to impressing peo-

32. www.goodreads.com/quotes/tag/aging (accessed April 3, 2014).

ple with their royal lifestyle. And all too often their single-minded love for the wife of their youth is compromised as they indulge in sexual exploits, use high-class prostitutes, or simply abandon their aging wife for a "new and younger model." We can see that in many Christians who start well (following Jesus in what Eugene Peterson calls "a long obedience in the same direction"), but all kinds of factors lead them to abandon that single-mindedness. How their own children have turned out (some good and some not so good), the influence of a pluralistic society, and close associates in business from other religious backgrounds lead to the dissolution of their faith. Sometimes they marry a second or third time outside their faith and get sucked into something other than loving the Lord God with all their heart, soul, strength, and mind.

Solomon is an example of this. He did not finish well. He finished as a compromised old man with a lustful mind, as is so clearly revealed in the Old Testament book the Song of Songs.[33] How did it happen for Solomon? We have much to learn negatively from his behavior. It happened in stages, not all at once, which is why young people need to plan to finish well.

A good example in Scripture — and part of the following study — as a contrast with Solomon is Samuel, the leader of Israel during the time of the judges. He was able to finish well. His last speech is a wonderful summary of his life and an inspiration to us. Finally, in the New Testament we have some of the final words of the apostle Paul as a goal.

Personal Reflection:

What would "finishing well" be like for you? Be as specific as possible.

---

33. This is not the place to expound the enigmatic book Song of Songs or Song of Solomon, but the best interpretation is that Solomon is in process of acquiring yet one more beautiful young woman for his harem. She, however, is already pledged to a shepherd lover to whom she goes either in dream or reality. Meanwhile Solomon "courts" her by reciting her anatomical advantages while the shepherd lover, in the end, says something like, "Solomon can have his harem but she is my one and only." It is a poem of the beauty of erotic love with covenant partners and disgust of Solomon's lust.

Group Discussion:

We all have stories of leaders who did not finish well. What have we learned from their examples to guide us in our own desire to finish this life triumphantly?

Read 1 Kings 10:14–11:13

1. The historical record says, "King Solomon was greater in riches and wisdom than all the other kings of the earth" (10:23). For all his wisdom in his younger years, what clues do we have of the flaws in Solomon's reign that led him to finish as a compromised old king?

2. Why is compromise in the area of sex so damaging to long-term integrity?

3. Why is compromise in money so damaging to long-term integrity?

4. To accomplish his massive building projects, Solomon used people as tools, and when he died they murdered his labor leader and the kingdom split in two. Why is compromise in power so damaging to long-term integrity?

5. Of the three that brought down Solomon — sex, money, and power — with which one do you struggle most?

6. How would you advise Solomon as a young man, if you had the opportunity, to conduct himself so that he would finish well?

Read 1 Samuel 12:1-5

7. This is the prophet-leader Samuel's final and farewell speech. Samuel has acted as a judge, a leader, and a teacher of the twelve tribes that occupied the Promised Land. Saul has been appointed king, and now Samuel can retire. What are the main things Samuel affirms about his own life?

8. What clues do we have that enabled him to finish well?

9. What would you like to be able to say at the end of your life?

Read 2 Timothy 4:6-8

10. What three things does Paul note about his finishing well? Translate these terms into attitudes and actions that we could emulate today.

11. It has often been suggested that those who finish well have determined this when they started well. What can you do at this point in your life to make sure you will finish as Samuel and Paul did?

"Let each man find out what God wants him to do, and then let him do it, or die in the attempt."

Charles Spurgeon[34]

34. Quoted from "An All-Round Ministry," in Larry J. Michael, *Spurgeon on Leadership* (Grand Rapids: Kregel, 2003), p. 67.

PART THREE

Legacy

....

7

Leaving a Multifaceted Legacy

How do you measure success? To laugh often and much; to win the respect of intelligent people and the affection of children; to earn the appreciation of honest critics and endure the betrayal of false friends; to appreciate beauty; to find the best in others; to leave the world a bit better, whether by a healthy child, a redeemed social condition, or a job well done; to know even one other life has breathed because you lived — this is to have succeeded.

Bessie Anderson Stanley[1]

Perhaps the most beautiful legacy that aging parents can leave their children is a personally lived lesson about facing old age and death with courage and grace.

Eugene Bianchi[2]

We want our lives to count, to leave something behind, or as Emerson put it, "to leave the world a bit better." We don't want to have an epitaph like Jehoram in the Old Testament, who "was thirty-two

---

1. This quotation, often wrongly attributed to Ralph Waldo Emerson, can be found at emerson-legacy.yamu.edu/Ephemera/success/html.
2. Eugene C. Bianchi, *Aging as a Spiritual Journey* (Eugene, OR: Wipf and Stock, 2011), p. 169.

years old when he became king, and he reigned in Jerusalem eight years. He passed away, to no one's regret" (2 Chron. 21:20). But our legacy is not merely the money we pass on to our family, if we are able to. It is a multifaceted and multigenerational contribution to the human race. This raises the question of what is true wealth and wealth that can be passed on. We will consider that topic, then the matter of a last will and testament, and will end the chapter with questions for reflection and a case study.

Legacy as Stewardship

The starting point is to acknowledge that we are not owners of anything but are stewards entrusted by the true owner, God, who has invested in us and expects us to invest what he has given. Jesus raises the challenge of this in his enigmatic answer to a trick question: whether he would pay taxes as a citizen of an occupied country to the hated Roman government. He said, "Give back to Caesar what is Caesar's, and to God what is God's" (Luke 20:25).

If all belongs to God, then what is given to Caesar and what is given to the temple can both be actions within and for the kingdom of God. Caesar support (read taxes and participation in civic, business, and social responsibilities) is not secular, and temple support (read supporting pastors and missionaries) is not exclusively sacred. Both can be kingdom actions. That is the *precondition* of kingdom stewardship. The actual *practice* of kingdom stewardship involves investment, and that is something the New Testament positively encourages.

Stewardship is not hoarding, not merely protecting an asset so it is not stolen. Stewardship is not squandering an asset on useless things or pleasures. It is investing as servants of the true owner, God, who holds us accountable for what we have done with what we have. But there is risk in this. We have a God who inspires innovation and risk taking. That is the message of the parable of the talents in Matthew 25:14-30, particularly in the judgment of the person who was entrusted with one talent, who did not invest it but kept it wrapped up in a handkerchief just as many people wrap up their lives in a sealed container.

Unlike the five-talent and two-talent persons, who made five and two more through shrewd investment, the one-talent man presented his one talent back. He had dug a hole in the ground and hid his master's money so it would not be stolen. Perhaps he thought he might be affirmed for keeping the talent intact. Instead he is terribly judged. As William Hendriksen puts it, "Jesus . . . is not opposed to responsible capitalism. Profit promotes employment and makes possible helping those in need."[3] But helping others was the last thing the one-talent person was thinking about. He was thinking about himself, lazing around in an orgy of leisure while the others were hard at work. "You wicked, lazy servant," the businessman says. The servant is fired. Worse, he is condemned. Why does he sustain such a terrible judgment? He did not throw away the talent. He did not squander it. He treasured it, kept it safe from robbers. But by not investing, that pitiable one-talent person lost everything — his one talent was given to the person with ten. Why? He had the wrong view of stewardship. He thought stewardship was preserving things intact, not investing.

He also had the wrong view of the businessman (read "God") — he thought the master was hard, harvesting where he had not sown and gathering where he had not scattered seed. So he says, "I was afraid" — afraid of losing it, afraid of the condemnation he might receive for not gaining anything, afraid of risk. The master says, if you really thought that of me — though in reality the businessman, who represents the Lord, was not this kind of person at all — then at least you should have entrusted my money with the bankers so it would have earned interest. Even in the ancient world there were bankers, who sat at a bench exchanging money and receiving coins or bags of gold and providing some interest, and doing so by lending that money at a higher rate of interest to others — not unlike our present banks. The one-talent man had a flawed view of God — a hard God who would zap him if he made a mistake. One cannot take a risk with a judging God, whereas the God and Father of Jesus Christ is a God who can even redeem our

---

3. William Hendriksen, *Exposition of the Gospel according to Matthew* (Grand Rapids: Baker Book House, 1973), p. 883.

mistakes. He inspires creativity and expects us to take risks. Let me illustrate this with a story.

Before our children left home we had the privilege of taking a backpacking trip to Europe and the Middle East. First we went to Greece and specifically to Delphi, where in ancient times people came to consult the will of the gods at the Delphic oracle.

In ancient Delphi a priestess sat on a tripod and, when asked, inhaled narcotic fumes from a fire below. If a king came from Sardis in Turkey and wanted to know whether he would win or lose the war he was about to undertake — a good thing to know — she would inhale the fumes and answer, "A great king will fall in the war," not specifying which one! If a pregnant woman came asking whether she was carrying a son or a daughter, the oracle would say, "Son, no, daughter." The will of the gods in ancient Greece was ambiguous.

Then we flew into Cairo. The man at the next table in a restaurant was sitting alone, obviously not a tourist.

"What are you, an American, doing in Cairo?"

"I am here for two years training the Egyptian fighter pilots on the F-16."

"That's fascinating. What is the biggest problem you face in your daily work?"

"My biggest problem is that when the red warning lights come on in the cockpit, they do nothing."

"Why do they do nothing?"

"They say, if it is the will of Allah for the plane to crash, it will crash."

We then crossed the desert in an Arab bus, past scrawny little communities with a few goats kept in a stockade of palm branches. But at the border with Israel (and I understand this is a complicated thing to say), we crossed into fruit trees laden with pomegranates, apricots, and lemons, swaying hay, and incredible creativity. How come? Because the will of God in both the Old and New Testament, the will of the God of Abraham, Isaac, and Jacob, and Jesus, is not ambiguous, as with the Greeks, and not inexorable, as within Islam, but an empowering vision of greatness under God, a dream, a prospect, and a personal presence that inspire initiative and investment. It is like the dream that God gave Joseph in the Old Testament.

So creating a legacy involves investing as stewards, and investing primarily in the kingdom of God.

Kingdom Legacy

The kingdom of God is a revolutionary perspective that in effect spells the end to both religion and secularism. The kingdom of God is not just spiritual and certainly not religious. It is the invasion of all of life with the *shalom*-bringing, life-enhancing rule of God. The kingdom was the master thought of Jesus. His first and last sermons on earth were about the kingdom.[4] He personally embodied the kingdom in his life and work — forgiving sins, touching the leper, grappling with the powers, bringing dignity to people, and making people whole. Jesus destroyed the dualism of sacred and secular that still pervades the church, namely, that certain actions, works, and places are sacred and others are secular.

I grew up on the poem "Only one life, twill soon be past, only what's done for Jesus will last," as though soul work is the only lasting investment. In time I will show that the poem is ironically true — only what's done for Jesus will last, whether stockbrokering, house building, selling, healing the body, homemaking, or pastoring. There is a very famous book which millions have read that contains so much wonderful truth that I hesitate to quote a "fatal flaw," which is this: the author says that in his church he has wealth builders and kingdom builders. And he persuades the wealth builders to make as much money as they can to invest in kingdom work, meaning preaching, Christian education, mission, evangelism, and so on.

Yes, it is a great thing to share the good news of Jesus with another. We are all called to do this. Yes, it is a wonderful thing to care for souls. All of us are called into the ministry, not just pastors. But the kingdom cannot be reduced to church work, to inner piety, or even to personal salvation. Jesus did not preach the gospel of soul salvation but the good news of the kingdom.[5] And this means that

4. Matt. 4:17; Acts 1:3.
5. Mortimer Arias, *Announcing the Kingdom: Evangelization and the Subversive Memory of Jesus* (Lima, OH: Academic Renewal Press, 1984), pp. 66-67.

we are building a kingdom legacy not only in stated ministry but also through good work done in the world.

Work is kingdom work when it creates new wealth, alleviates poverty, brings well-being to people, embellishes and improves human life, engages powers resistant to God's coming *shalom*, and brings people under the life-giving rule of God in their lives. René Padilla, a South American theologian, says, "All human work that embodies Kingdom values and serves Kingdom goals can be rightly termed as Kingdom ministry. Gospel work and so-called 'secular work' are actually interdependent."[6] The line between "sacred" and "secular" is erased in the kingdom of God. All things are within the sphere of God's sovereignty and therefore God's concern.

And kingdom work will last, will be purged of sin at the second coming of Jesus, and will find its place in the new heaven and new earth. So in the end, the question asked by God in evaluating our lives will not be how much soul-work we did in this life. But first, do I know you? Do we have a relationship? Will he say, "I know you"?[7] And then, a second question, What did you do with what I gave you? This raises the important question of what money is and what it means.

Kingdom Money

Important spiritual questions are raised by money. From the beginning of Christian history church leaders have recognized that economic life is an incarnation of the spiritual life. But the Bible seems to have two voices on money: it is both a blessing and a curse. The French philosopher Jacques Ellul notes that the Old Testament regarded wealth as a *blessing* (Deut. 30:9) — though the exemplars, Abraham, Job, and Solomon, depended on God rather than their wealth.[8] Money is a *sacrament* as God is the giver of wealth (1 Sam.

---

6. René Padilla, "The Mission of the Church in the Light of the Kingdom of God," *Transformation* 1, no. 2 (April-June 1984): 19.

7. Matt. 7:23; 25:12.

8. Gen. 13:8-18; Job 1:21.

2:7-8; Eccles. 5:19). This also produces what Ellul calls "the scandal of wealth," whereby God sometimes gives wealth to the wicked.[9] Money is also a temptation. The pursuit of wealth for its own sake is a vain, destructive thing leading to self-destructive autonomy (Prov. 30:8; Hos. 12:8). Wealth is an *illusionary* security and will not satisfy (Eccles. 5:10).

In the New Testament there are dark warnings: the rich are accursed; riches can be the wages of sin and unrighteousness, especially toward the poor, with whom God takes his stand against the rich. Money too easily becomes an alternative God ("mammon," which means firmness and stability).[10] According to Jesus, "You cannot serve both God and Money" (Matt. 6:24). It is not neutral. It has an ability to inspire devotion and shares many of the characteristics of deity — giving security, freedom, and power.[11] "The Almighty Dollar" is a power (Eph. 1:21). Jesus calls it "wicked Mammon" (KJV) or "worldly wealth" (TNIV). And Paul says the "love of money is a root of all kinds of evil" (1 Tim. 6:10). The Old Testament blessing "May the Lord bless you and keep you" (Num. 6:24) has been understood by Jewish people as follows: "'May the Lord bless you' means 'to be blessed with wealth and possessions,' and 'May God keep you' means 'May God keep your wealth and possessions from possessing you.'"[12]

Can the two voices of Scripture be heard as one harmonious word from God? J. Schneider affirms this harmony as we seek first the kingdom of God. "What really matters is that our economic lives spring forth from souls neither too withered for delight nor too hard for compassion."[13] First, our handling of money is revelatory of the state of our souls. Are we pinched misers, extravagant givers,

---

9. Ps. 73:12-13; Job 21:7-21.

10. Jacques Ellul, *Money and Power*, trans. LaVonne Neff (Downers Grove, IL: InterVarsity Press, 1984).

11. Richard Foster, *Money, Sex, and Power: The Challenge of the Disciplined Life* (New York: Harper and Row, 1985), p. 28.

12. Jeffrey K. Salkin, *Being God's Partner: How to Find the Hidden Link between Spirituality and Work* (Woodstock, VT: Jewish Lights Publishing), p. 162.

13. J. Schneider, "Money," in Robert Banks and R. Paul Stevens, eds., *The Complete Book of Everyday Christianity* (Downers Grove, IL: InterVarsity Press, 1997), p. 662.

grateful stewards finding prayer and worship around both giving and receiving? Second, our use of money invites dependence on God, who is the provider of everything we need. Behind this is the spiritual discipline of relinquishing ownership to God and practicing thanksgiving. Third, by giving to others we "profane Mammon" (Ellul's phrase) and liberate money for sacramental purposes. This happens especially when we give to the poor with no strings attached (2 Cor. 9:7) and give generously as the Spirit enables (Rom. 12:8). Fourth, we are invited to practice some form of voluntary impoverishment (Acts 4:35-37). Finally, if so directed, we are called to sell all and follow Jesus.

David Hataj took over his father's precision and custom gear business. With entrepreneurial skill he moved that business from a small shop in Wisconsin to a major business that does custom gear manufacturing for printing presses and food-making machines, just to name a couple of applications. Their service is so good that David does not spend a dollar on advertising. Recently he even posted on his Web site that he cannot take on any new customers for the time being. His earnings from this and two other businesses he has started have skyrocketed. But David and his wife Tracy decided at the very beginning to peg their income and lifestyle to a certain dollar amount. And they continue to live that way eighteen years after taking over the business, thus freeing up a large amount of money for reinvestment in the business and many wonderful projects that David has developed in needier parts of the world.

John Wesley in his sermon "The Use of Money" famously said, "Gain all you can, save all you can, give all you can."[14] It is all God's. Gain as much as you can without manipulating others or abusing your own body. Be creative and innovative. Work hard. But save all you can. That money too is God's resource tucked away in a bank account or under the mattress. And then give all you can. All of it is a kingdom resource, not just the part dedicated to specifically Christian enterprises.

---

14. John Wesley, "The Use of Money," in Max L. Stackhouse et al., eds., *On Moral Business: Classical and Contemporary Resources for Ethics in Economic Life* (Grand Rapids: Eerdmans, 1995), pp. 194-97.

Nonmonetary Kingdom Investments

So the central biblical concept of the kingdom of God provides a liberating perspective on how we can create a legacy through investment of ourselves. We have explored our kingdom stewardship of money. But there is more.

Investing in People

Kingdom stewards contribute to the well-being of others through education, undertaking good work, inventing and innovating new products and services, and giving direct assistance to others and helping people to be reconciled with each other and their Creator.

There is an extraordinary statement in the Gospel of Luke in a little expounded chapter (16). In this chapter Jesus tells the story of a person who was rich and did not care for the poor man begging at his gate. The rich and the poor both died, but the rich person went to Hades and the poor man went to the bosom of Abraham, a figure of speech for Jewish heaven. The secret of this great separation is not that one person was rich and the other poor; the secret is in the name of the poor man: Lazarus means "God is my helper." The rich man was self-sufficient and did not care for his neighbor. In hell he pleads that someone, even poor Lazarus, would return and warn his five rich brothers of their fate.

The chapter begins with a different story. This one is about a manager who is about to be fired. The manager goes to his boss's creditors and arranges for the reduction of their loan by a significant percentage, almost half. This may well be the exorbitant interest that was wrongly charged by the boss who, as a Jew, was not supposed to lend money with interest. At any rate, when the manager lost his job these new friends took him into their homes. Then Jesus says something outrageous. "I tell you, use worldly wealth to gain friends for yourselves, so that when it is gone, you will be welcomed into eternal dwellings" (Luke 16:9). Jesus is not saying to "buy" friendship with your money but rather to use money in such a way that you have gained friends that will last forever. It is a stunning statement for the aging especially. Here is why.

The only treasure we can take from this life to the next is the relationships we have made through Christ. No armored vehicle ever follows a hearse to the cemetery. You can't take it with you: the car, the house, the jewels, or the cash. But what you do take are relationships, friends in Jesus and the friends of Jesus. And this is a process of spiritual formation that is evoked by aging. Our real legacy, the only lasting inheritance we have, is social and spiritual. As we have seen, aging is a process of progressive relinquishment: first we give up the omnipotence of youth, then perfect health, then family members and parents (who die), usually remunerated employment and our careers, followed by our driver's license and physical strength as frailty increases. In the end we are left with the only treasure we can take with us, Jesus, and the forever family of God. This neighbor principle is further elaborated in Luke 14:12-14, where Jesus counsels us to show hospitality to those who cannot repay us. In so speaking he points us to another way of kingdom stewardship and creating a legacy.

Investing in the Poor

In a series of sermons on Luke 16, the early church father John Chrysostom said that wealth is given to the rich as stewards for the poor (Prov. 31:5, 8, 9).[15] Just how do we do this? The medieval Jew Maimonides (Moses ben Maimon, 1135-1204) defined charity's eight degrees by ranking them. The lowest level is giving with regret or reluctance: a gift of the hand and not of the heart. The highest is this:

> Lastly . . . the most meritorious of all, is to anticipate charity, by preventing poverty; namely, to assist the reduced brother, either by a considerable gift, or a loan of money, or by teaching him a trade, or by putting him in the way of business, so that he may earn an honest livelihood; and not be forced to the dreadful alternative of holding up his hand for charity. This is the highest step and the summit of charity's Golden Ladder.[16]

15. John Chrysostom, *On Wealth and Poverty*, trans. Catherine P. Roth (Crestwood, NY: St. Vladimir's Seminary Press, 1984), p. 12.
16. H. Hurwitz, *The Ancient Hebrew Sages* (Morrison and Watt, 1826); www.sofii.org/node/820 (accessed January 17, 2013).

Wonderfully this is being done today not only through microeconomic development but also by larger enterprises, especially through work like that being done by Dr. Kim Tan and many others who argue that enterprise, not aid, is the best way to relieve poverty.[17] So now we come to developing instruments to pass on our multifaceted legacy to invest in the next generation, particularly in terms of money and material assets.

Material Investing in the Next Generation[18]

One of the most sensitive things we do in life is to write a last will and testament. A will can be a family blessing, a form of gift giving, and a means of bringing peace and justice to our families. It can bless charitable organizations and encourage causes we embraced in this life. It can also be a hand extending from the grave to control, manipulate, divide, and bring retribution for wounds not healed before we died. In that regard, a will reveals not only the state of our financial assets but also the state of our souls. Some people do not bother to make a will, not so much for "spiritual" reasons or even because their assets are comparatively small, but because they do not think it important. They do not survive, of course, to see people fighting over their possessions or the hurts caused by people assuming they were the proper heirs but not actually receiving the promised inheritance.

It is not the purpose of this chapter to advise how a will should be written. Normally this should be done by a lawyer, though simple forms can be obtained in banks and elsewhere, which can be legal, if properly witnessed by two adults who are not beneficiaries, and correctly signed and dated. Properly conceived, wills name the executor (the person named to administer the will) and the beneficiaries (those who receive specific portions of the estate). They also need

---

17. Brian Griffiths and Kim Tan, *Fighting Poverty through Enterprise: The Case for Social Venture Capital* (Coventry, UK: Transformational Business Network, 2007).

18. Some of the following was published in R. Paul Stevens, "Will, Last," in Banks and Stevens, *The Complete Book of Everyday Christianity*, pp. 1117-20.

to be updated every five years or when there has been a change of residence, marital status, or family circumstances. My purpose here is to explore the meaning of writing a will. It is not always, however, a loving ministry or a way of creating a positive legacy.

The Will to Curse

While the saying "You can't take it with you" is undoubtedly true, it is possible to extend a hand beyond the grave and wreak havoc on a family. Some people use their wills to control people they were unable to control in this life. In 1558 Michael Wentworth specified in his will that "if any of my daughters will not be advised by my executors, but of their own fantastical brain bestow themselves lightly upon a light person [deemed an unsuitable marriage partner], then that daughter was to have only sixty-six pounds instead of the one hundred pounds which was promised to the obedient."[19] This has been rightly judged to be posthumous economic blackmail.

A son or daughter may be out of favor or may have disgraced the family. Further wounds are inflicted posthumously by disinheriting that child, though the law sometimes precludes totally excluding a near relative simply because that person was not named in the will. No one dies with all the problems in his or her family fully resolved. Someone is loved less; someone is struggling with addiction and would possibly squander an inheritance; someone is idle and lazy; someone has wounded or shamed the family. Not surprisingly, some people use the will as their last chance to "get even," without remaining to assist in picking up the pieces. Rightly understood, making a will is an act of stewardship — undertaking to manage one's household and appropriately transferring ownership and responsibility. When a child is incompetent or foolish, a lawyer can assist in specifying a trust fund. Last wills cannot do much to solve family problems, but when poorly conceived, they can exacerbate the ones that already exist.

19. L. Stone, "The Rise of the Nuclear Family," in C. E. Rosenburg, ed., *The Family in History* (Philadelphia: University of Pennsylvania Press, 1975), p. 46.

The Will to Bless

Normally a will should express justice and fairness in a family. This is not easy when there are great differences in economic strength among surviving members. It may be tempting to write a will based on perceived need rather than fairness: "James doesn't need my money since he has a professional income, but poor Martha has never had a chance." What the person cannot foresee are the reverses of life: James struggling with an incurable disease and unable to work; Martha divorced and remarried into a wealthy family. The case study below raises these questions. Further, it is impossible to regulate people's feelings. The elder son in the parable of the prodigal complained, "You never gave me" — when the father had given him everything (Luke 15:29, 31)! But what we can do in writing a will is to refuse to play favorites, to express mercy on those who have disappointed us, to provide as best we can for all kin who survive us, and to trust that God will help them deal with such ongoing temptations of life as envy, greed, and covetousness.

As a form of gift giving, a last will can do a lot of good. First, if we have a surviving spouse, he or she will be able to continue a reasonably normal life. It is a practical way of loving our spouse. Second, we can continue our priorities in parenting by naming a suitable guardian (with his or her permission) for our minor-aged children and providing for their maintenance. Third, we can bring positive delight to people by specifying the transfer of possessions that will bring joy to a particular relative or friend. For example, we can imagine that mahogany table, which Linda always loved, now in her living room. Fourth, we can empower the next generation to do things they would not otherwise be able to do, such as buying their own home. Fifth, we can see that all the outstanding debts in this life, relational and financial, are forgiven. Sixth, we can bless charities and churches with a significant gift. Seventh, we can show impartial love like God's love to every member of the family, regardless of merit and performance, just as God makes the sun to rise on the just and unjust (Matt. 5:43-47).

The Living Will

Many people today write a living will in addition to the one to be executed upon their death. A *living will* outlines how a person wants to be medically treated in the event of a terminal illness or a condition that requires life-sustaining procedures. The admitting office of a hospital is not a time and place to determine whether certain life-sustaining procedures should be undertaken. My father arrived at the hospital, suffering from a total second stroke, and my mother, when asked, determined that he would be fed by a gastric tube, which he was for two years. It is normally a gracious thing to do this, as close members of the family, without such direction, may feel obliged to prolong life as long as possible, fearing accusations of disloyalty or lack of love. A living will too can be drawn up by a lawyer. While some people think this is a means of *causing* death, it really is a way of regulating the unnecessary delay of death through heroic medical interventions. Christians especially should be prepared to die. Making a living will helps us to prepare for our death and to continue the process of relinquishment, which is a spiritual discipline. This is both a ministry to ourselves (and not a selfish one) and a ministry to our survivors at the same time.[20] But there is more to be passed on than money and things.

The Ethical Will

In the long Judeo-Christian tradition, many people have left an "ethical will." An ethical will (Hebrew: *Zava'ah*) is a document designed to pass ethical values from one generation to the next. Rabbis and Jewish laypeople wrote ethical wills during the nineteenth and twentieth centuries. In recent years, the practice has been more widely used by the general public. In *Business Week* magazine and in an American Bar Association electronic newsletter, it is described as an aid to estate planning.

This could be done in a letter to one's family, or even as part of the last will. Some people write their family stories in words or pictures or both as a way of passing on the values considered to be

---

20. See "The Practice of Advance Directives," in Allen Verhey, *The Christian Art of Dying: Learning from Jesus* (Grand Rapids: Eerdmans, 2011), pp. 357-63.

crucial to thriving morally and spiritually in the next generation. My friend Alec Woodhull has taken some years to assemble his family stories, and their moral and spiritual meaning, in what he calls his "Alligator Tales," coming as he does from Florida and growing up, as he says, "with sand between his toes."

The earth, the traditions of culture and family, the material and spiritual treasures of one's family — these are not for ourselves alone but for our children and children's children (Prov. 13:22; compare Ps. 17:14).

So what do you plan to leave behind? Will it be true wealth? The questions below can help us reflect on this multigenerational and multifaceted inheritance.[21] First, we can contribute to a kingdom which will never end, but will be transformed at the coming of Christ. Some of our work in this world will survive and be transfigured (1 Cor. 15:58). Second, we can belong to a "forever family" of relationships in Christ which will transcend death. Third, we can create a multigenerational inheritance of values, virtues, purposes, experiences, work, and material assets that can be passed on to others as a blessing. Fourth, a great treasure, if not the greatest, is knowing and loving God and being known and loved by God. While we cannot actually pass this on, we can point to its inestimable value. The same is true for the next dimension of true wealth. Fifth, we can experience joy and peace in God. Finally, we have the treasure of a wonderful and certain destiny, a future with hope and promise that will outlast this world and this life, the new heaven and the new earth. This is our true legacy, and much of it can be passed on to the next generation.

---

21. Other resources are R. Paul Stevens, "Stewardship," in Banks and Stevens, *The Complete Book of Everyday Christianity*, pp. 962-67; R. Paul Stevens and Alvin Ung, "Joyful Relinquishment" and "Surrendered Contentment," in *Taking Your Soul to Work: Overcoming the Nine Deadly Sins of the Workplace* (Grand Rapids: Eerdmans, 2010), pp. 139-50; Laura Nash and Howard Stevenson, *Just Enough: Tools for Creating Success in Your Work and Life* (Hoboken, NJ: Wiley and Sons, 2004).

Questions for Reflection

1. What are the values and virtues you would like to leave behind?
2. If you could write an epitaph for your grave (and have lots of space to write it!), what would you like to say?
3. Reflect on the last will in each family in the following case study.

Samuel and Edna

Samuel is a pilot with Air Canada. While he lives today in a fine home and has two cars and a boat, he started off in poverty and worked his way up, initially flying as a bush pilot wherever he could get work. He has two children; both are now grown and have left home. During their teen years he often reminded them that he "made it" by hard work and they needed to do the same thing. So he did not help them with university fees and, upon completion of high school, charged them rent if they decided to live at home — though the "rent" was much less than the going rate. Samuel is quite open about the fact that he and his wife Rachel will spend almost everything they have before they die, much of it in generous gifts to Christian causes and to supporting Christian missionaries. They hope to have nothing left in their estate by the time they die, especially since one of their sons is an alcoholic. Their reasoning, following that of Andrew Carnegie (the American billionaire), is that wealth should be administered by its possessors during their lifetime. Samuel's reasons (parallel with Carnegie's) were these: (1) a large legacy is a disaster for those receiving it; (2) it tends to breed weakness, dependency, and uncreative lives.

Edna was a lawyer, though she is now retired and has been widowed for almost a decade. With the combined assets of her husband's work as a university professor and her own legal career, she plans to leave as much as she can to her three children, two of whom are married and the third living contentedly single. The single child is a professional, owns two mountain bikes, a BMW, and lives from expensive vacation to vacation — having no perceivable financial need. In contrast, the two married children (each with two children) are struggling to obtain a small home in the distant suburbs of the city. Edna is planning to sell her lovely home, live in a small apartment, and pass on much of the proceeds of the sale to her two married children, to help with a home purchase. After all, Jonathan, the single, has no apparent need. The same holds true for the will, which reads that four-fifths of all assets are to be dispersed to the married children and only one-fifth is to be divided between the single son and her home church. All three of the children complain to her that she should be enjoying life now rather than saving it all up for her children.

Which will best reflects a Christian view of stewardship?

Personal or Group Study: Late Life Legacy Work: Genesis 47:28-31; 48:1-22; 49:29–50:3

We return to the story of Jacob mentioned in chapter 3. In ancient times the equivalent of the last will was the father's oral blessing of the family before he died. Isaac blessing Esau, his older son, in contradiction to God's revealed plan of maintaining the family leadership through Jacob (Gen. 25:23), is a classic story of a last will gone awry. Sometimes the inheritance could be gained in advance, as witnessed by the younger son's request in the parable of the prodigal (Luke 15:11-32). But there are even more important things to have settled than finances and funeral arrangements, and they arise in the passage we are studying. It is critical that we are able to die with relationships healed as much as possible. A pastor of our church visiting with a member of our small group who was soon to die asked, "Is there anyone with whom you have a broken relationship that needs to be healed?" She was able to answer in the negative. But it is unusual. And there is also one's own conscience, spirit, and heart. Are we at peace with God, our sins forgiven, and in right relationship not only with our neighbors but with our Maker? The patriarch Jacob's story is profoundly revealing of so many aspects of everyday life and everyday spirituality but supremely on the matter of late life work, preparing for the ultimate leave-taking.[22]

Personal Reflection:
Do you find it hard to think about and plan for your own death? Why? Your own passing may be a long way off or it may be near. What have you done to prepare yourself for it?

Group Discussion:
Why do people find it so hard to talk about death, and specifically their own death?

Read Genesis 47:28-31

1. What arrangements does Jacob make for his own burial? Why was it so important for him not to be buried in Egypt?
2. Is the place where you are to be buried or your ashes spread important to you? Why?

Read Genesis 48:1-22

3. This is a scene of family blessing, passing on the leadership of the tribe and the entitlements of the next generation. Jacob has moved down to Egypt where his son Joseph is second in command. But Jacob is ill and about to die. Why do you think Jacob reviews his own life story and spiritual journey at this point (vv. 3-4, see also vv. 21-22)?
4. Have you shared your own spiritual journey with your children and grandchildren (if you have them)? Why or why not? If so, how much have you shared?
5. What provision does Jacob make for the leadership of the family? Note that Jacob does not merely bless his grandchildren Manasseh and Ephraim but adopts them as his sons along with the other twelve (v. 5)?
6. What "death work" does it seem Jacob is doing here?[23]

---

22. See R. Paul Stevens, *Down-to-Earth Spirituality: Encountering God in the Ordinary, Boring Stuff of Life* (Downers Grove, IL: InterVarsity Press, 2003), pp. 166-81.
23. See footnotes 17-18 in chapter 3.

Read Genesis 49:29–50:3

7. What indicates that Jacob died in peace in right relations with God and neighbor?

8. The Bible notes that the fear of death holds people in lifelong bondage (Heb. 2:15). Why do you think this is so? Do you think Christian faith eliminates this fear or changes it (see Rom. 8:39)?

9. Is there late-life work you need to do? If so, what is it?

"The Christian approach is to regard readiness to die as the first step in learning to live."

J. I. Packer[24]

Now or Later:

For discussion: Do you think providing a "living will" that specifies what extraordinary life-prolonging medical procedures one does not wish is a Christian approach to death?

24. Quoted in T. K. Jones, "Death: Real Meaning in Life Is to Be Found beyond Life," *Christianity Today* 35 (June 24, 1991): 30.

8

Life Review and Life Preview

Life review for the elderly is not sufficient; they must also engage in a "life preview."

Eugene Bianchi[1]

We can think of aging as a kind of "natural monastery" in which earlier roles, attachments, and pleasures are naturally stripped away from us.

Zalman Schachter-Shalomi[2]

Brian, a dear friend, died of ALS, a progressively debilitating disease in which the person gradually loses all bodily functions. I had asked Brian for permission to share his journals from his book called *Closing Comments.* Here is one of his journal entries:

> Lately, I have had a few fits of minor depression when I face the limits of my life. This disease isolates one from so much. I would like to think that I still have some usefulness. But I must ·

1. Eugene C. Bianchi, *Aging as a Spiritual Journey* (Eugene, OR: Wipf and Stock, 2011), p. 207.

2. Zalman Schachter-Shalomi, *From Age-ing to Sage-ing: A Profound New Vision of Growing Older* (New York: Grand Central Publishing, 1995), p. 26.

find ways of being useful outside of areas that I normally was productive in.

Sometimes I feel sorry for myself. But it doesn't do much good. I think most of the time I accept the gift of tranquility as an adequate offset to all the activity and running around that I am missing. The shortness of life is something we all should face every day and do the most with what we have today. Because of my condition I spend time wondering what the transition will be between this life and the next. It is a wonderful mystery, and one which at times I even doubt. But in the end I rely on the scriptural promises and my limited understanding of the new creation which only a loving God could have imagined. What do we have without Jesus, "the radiance of God's glory and the exact representation of his being"?

After we visited the respirologist today we visited an ALS friend at VGH who went on a respirator just before Christmas and still is not out of the hospital from various complications. If I continue to do well with my speaking ability and have some arm and leg mobility I think I will continue as I am. But if I were to find myself in the condition that he appears to be in I think I would rally my troops around and say my farewells. There are too many scriptural images of life with the everlasting Father and Son for me to want to endure the effort that we would all need to exert for me to cling to the bottom (or is it the top?) rung of this earthly ladder.

But how do I really know what I would do? What is it that makes us want to hang on so hard?

Well, I know some reasons. One just came and kissed me.[3]

He was prepared to die. Indeed, he had lots of time to do it. But were the Puritans right, after all, that life is lived best if we prepare for death, even if we do not have a lingering terminal illness? David Stannard opines, "The Puritans infused aging with a wealth of social and religious meaning. They encouraged even the oldest individ-

3. Brian A. Smith, *Closing Comments: ALS — a Spiritual Journey into the Heart of a Fatal Affliction* (Toronto: Clements Publishing, 2000), pp. 121-22.

ual to cherish each moment of life while preparing to relinquish it. Living on the edge of uncertainty about both their earthly and their eternal fate, Puritans of all ages faced death 'with the intensity virtually unknown in modern American life.'[4] Not only the Puritans but also the long tradition of the church prior to the Protestant Reformation has encouraged preparation for death while we are living. Typical of this are the words of Erasmus: "This preparation for death must be practiced through our whole life, and the spark of faith must be continually fanned so that it grows and gains strength."[5]

Extrapolating on his own experience, Dwight Small says, "Sometimes the feeling of futility in retirement lies in trying 'to feel at home in this world.' Retirement might better be a time when we wean ourselves from assuming that our destiny resides in anything realized in this passing world. How truly Goethe observed that 'those who do not hope for another life are always dead to this one.'"[6] Malcolm Muggeridge, the former editor of *Punch*, famously said, "The only ultimate disaster that can befall us, I have come to realize, is to feel ourselves to be at home here on earth. As long as we are aliens, we cannot forget our true homeland."[7] And C. S. Lewis, on the same line of thought, said, "If I find in myself a desire which no experience in the world can satisfy, the most probable explanation is that I was made for another world."[8]

So just how can we prepare for a good death?[9] We have already

4. Quoted in Carol Bailey Stoneking, "Modernity: The Social Construction of Aging," in Stanley Hauerwas et al., eds., *Growing Old in Christ* (Grand Rapids: Eerdmans, 2003), p. 76.

5. Erasmus, "Preparing for Death" (1553), in John W. O'Malley, ed., *Collected Works of Erasmus: Spiritualia and Pastoralia* (Toronto: University of Toronto Press, 1998), pp. 392-430, quoted in Allen Verhey, *The Christian Art of Dying: Learning from Jesus* (Grand Rapids: Eerdmans, 2011), p. 255.

6. Dwight Hervey Small, *When Christians Retire: Finding New Purpose in Your Bonus Years* (Kansas City, MO: Beacon Hill Press, 2000), p. 113.

7. Small, *When Christians Retire*, p. 122.

8. C. S. Lewis, *Mere Christianity* (London: Geoffrey Bles, 1953), p. 120.

9. See the chapter "A Good Dying," in Fred Craddock, Dale Goldsmith, and Joy V. Goldsmith, *Speaking of Dying: Recovering the Church's Voice in the Face of Death* (Grand Rapids: Brazos Press, 2012), pp. 163-94. In particular, these authors outline much of what the church can do to help people die well.

considered preparing a multifaceted and multigenerational legacy to be left after we die. The starting point is to repudiate the death denial of our contemporary Western culture. But there is more.

Preparing for Death

First, we need to live with the idea of dual citizenship: living simultaneously in this world and the next. We are equidistant from eternity every moment of our lives, from conception to resurrection. We treasure life as good and really flourish on earth, but it is not the highest good. We resist death as evil, but not the greatest evil, because it is the way to a better world. As we will see in the study on Psalm 90 at the end of this chapter, this involves numbering our days, as the psalmist said, by not calculating our expected life span by the latest actuarial tables and then squeezing all we can into the remaining years because there is nothing more (or because eternity is just more of the same). This view unfortunately treats time as a resource to be managed rather than a gift. Numbering our days means treating every day as a gift, being aware that it may be our last yet investing ourselves, talents and all, in a world without end (compare Matt. 25:1-13). Luther is famously quoted as saying, "If I knew that tomorrow the world would perish, I would still plant a little apple tree today in my backyard."[10] We do not live "on borrowed time" but on entrusted time. So we live one day at a time, not bearing tomorrow's burdens and anxieties today (Matt. 6:25-34), but trusting that God will be sufficient for each day that we live.

Second, we should practice the discipline of continuous learning. "The greatest tragedy for a religious person," says Eugene Bianchi, "is not being a sinner, but the embracing of stagnation, the refusal to grow."[11] Reuel Howe adds, "You don't grow old; when you cease to grow you are old."[12]

10. While this is attributed to Luther, it may stem from a grenadier of Frederick II of Prussia. Markus Barth, *Ephesians 4-6*, Anchor Bible (Garden City, NY: Doubleday and Co., 1960), p. 517.

11. Bianchi, *Aging as a Spiritual Journey*, pp. 57-58.

12. Quoted in Bianchi, *Aging as a Spiritual Journey*, p. 194.

The fact is that these life transitions are challenging and sometimes painful, but they also can be the most significant growing moments of our lives, especially if we do not simply give up work and indulge in an orgy of leisure until we have played and consumed ourselves to death. On this point Richard Bolles in his *Three Boxes of Life* makes a telling point. He notes that people tend to live their lives in three boxes: the first twenty years in study, the next forty years in work, and the last twenty years in play. What we need to do, Bolles suggests, is study, work, and play simultaneously to the end; and the end, as we have seen, may be another new beginning when we will study, worship, work, and play in the new heaven and new earth.

I was called into the hospice to visit my friend Angus who was dying. I expected to find him not able to communicate. What I found was a book beside his bed which he was actively reading and digesting, the contents of which he enthusiastically shared with me. He was a learner to the grave.

So why study when the major part of your career development is over and you are now freer to do, as my friend Charles Ringma says, "whatever you love"? The question could also be asked about the next life: one Roman Catholic theologian confessed that he was bored with the thought of going to heaven. If heaven is all growth and development, as pithily suggested by the image in Revelation that the leaves of the tree of life beside the river of life were for the "healing of the nations" (Rev. 22:2), what needs to be healed? And what if growth in this life is a sign of being alive even if many of our physical cells are dying? But what if as persons we are becoming more alive, more interested and more helpful to others than ever before? "As St. Gregory of Nyssa already said in the fourth century, 'Sin happens whenever we refuse to keep growing.'"[13]

My late father-in-law, Stan Boulter, is a wonderful example of this. I previously mentioned that in his first retirement he became the leader of the process of converting rape seed into Canola, a now almost universal cooking oil. To the day of his death he not only

---

13. Quoted in Richard Rohr, *Falling Upward: A Spirituality for the Two Halves of Life* (San Francisco: Jossey-Bass, 2011), p. 51.

kept up on world events in the news, but enriched himself with reading, conversations, and exploring new frontiers. When great grandchildren visited, he would ply them with questions to learn what they were learning and to help them integrate it into their lives. In social contexts he was an engaging conversationalist. Earlier in his life (he did live to ninety-eight), in what we call "midlife," he took courses and gained an additional degree. While I was a theological student and used to visit his home — to see his daughter, of course — he would ply me with theological questions, often well beyond what I had already studied.

So in both public and private universities, as well as theological colleges, one of the greatest opportunities for growth is offering resources for lifelong learning to seniors. Yes, seniors may take longer to appropriate some truths, but they bring to their study a wealth of personal experience. Many groups of seniors enjoy clubs that watch DVDs of great lecture courses now available. I have heard of a church in Taiwan that offers a noncredential degree program for older people who take a stated number of courses. Many form book clubs. My wife belongs to one of these and has become a more interesting conversationalist. Personally, I find rereading some of the great books that have enriched my life a special joy. Tournier notes, "When one grows old, as Mauriac remarks, I believe one finds a special pleasure in re-reading old books one has read in the past."[14]

To keep learning we need to sign up for courses, attend Elderhostel events, get DVDs of great courses and great books, develop book clubs, and engage in a community of learners. Charles Ringma in Brisbane, Australia, hosts a theology discussion group in which people read major theological works, one a month, and then over tea or coffee in a home, the group discusses them. If we keep working, at least on some level, and keep learning, and keep playing, we are more likely to end well.

Third, we can practice progressive relinquishment. As we go through life, we relinquish childhood and youth, our friends and parents through death, our children as they leave home, and even-

---

14. Paul Tournier, *Learn to Grow Old,* trans. Edwin Hudson (Louisville: Westminster John Knox Press, 1991), p. 33.

tually our occupations and health. Most people will discover the hard words of the marriage vow, "until death us do part." As we grow older, we have to relinquish the sexual virility that we once had. This does not mean that we cease to be sexual persons or that intimacy and sexual companionship with the wife or husband of our youth cannot be experienced; indeed, there is nothing better than mature love. At some point we have to relinquish our careers, even if we find a way of working until we die, something which I commend. Prayer is one "work" that we can do until our last breath. Ultimately we must relinquish life in this world. We are left with the one treasure of inestimable value — the Lord. A person who is no longer able to work for health reasons can in a sense add even more "value" to the kingdom because now he is free to give himself fully to prayer.

Fourth, we can allow everyday hardships to give us an opportunity to learn to "die daily." Paul said that we are like sheep led daily to the slaughter. Through these pains, persecutions, and weaknesses that we suffer, we are able to live in the resurrection power of Christ, dying to self, living in him (2 Cor. 4:10-12, 16-18).

One of the Ignatian exercises invites us to contemplate our own death using our inspired imaginations, doing so prayerfully in the Lord's presence: people gathering around our bed, the funeral, the burial in the soil, the gradual decomposition of our body until all that we were as a person in this life has dissolved and we are ready for full transfiguration.[15] Are we ready to die? Are there broken relationships to be mended, persons to be forgiven, debts to settle? Is there something we can do for someone that we have been putting off?

Paul Tournier puts it clearly: "Retirement . . . has a quality of finality about it, like death. Moreover, it is only through a series of definitive renunciations that a man becomes aware that he has grown old."[16] It is these definitive renunciations that we must accept. The failure to accept them can easily lead to bitterness, and we could end our lives as cranky old men or women. Earlier I mentioned one

---

15. Anthony de Mello, S.J., *Sadhana: A Way to God* (Anand, India: Gujarat Sahitya Prakash, 1978), pp. 89-90.

16. Tournier, *Learn to Grow Old*, p. 171.

obvious renunciation, the loss of friends and family through death, through which we will always feel less complete. Speaking of the death of his friend, St. Augustine said, "I wondered yet more that myself, who was to him a second self, could live, he being dead."[17] Add to that the renunciation of near perfect health with increased restriction of mobility, hearing, eyesight, and even memory. Then, for those who have had the privilege of raising children, we feel we did not fulfill our mission with them, and they may not have turned out as we expected, almost certainly did not. It is the loss of the dream of perfect children. Letting go of a challenging career is a kind of death, and one that, if not accepted, can lead to vocational bitterness. Finally, there is the acceptance of death.

Some of the losses are tangible — job, colleagues, spouse, children who leave home. Some losses are intangible — dignity, status, hope, and possible love. Judith Viorst in *Necessary Losses* explains:

> Losing is the price we pay for living. It is also the source of much of our growth and gain. Making our way from birth to death, we also have to make our way through the pain of giving up and giving up and giving up. . . . And in confronting the many losses that are brought by time and death, we become a mourning and adapting self, finding at every stage — until we draw our final breath — opportunities for creative transformations.[18]

Critical to this process is lament, recorded by David in the Psalms. Other poets also expressed their grief, and sometimes even their rage, that things were turning out badly. Far from seeing this as a lack of faith, the Psalms puts this in the context of faith. They are expressing their losses to God. This is good therapy. Even Jesus lamented over Jerusalem, thus revealing his true humanity. Indeed, we can and do enter into the demise and death of Jesus.[19] This all depends on a very difficult discipline.

17. Quoted in Tournier, *Learn to Grow Old*, p. 172.
18. Quoted in Small, *When Christians Retire*, p. 40.
19. Craddock, Goldsmith, and Goldsmith, *Speaking of Dying*, p. 137. In a section titled "What the Dying Might Want to Say," the authors draw on the experience of

Finally, we can practice the radical discipline of acceptance as we face progressive diminishment. Brian Smith, with whose reflections we began this chapter, talks about the loss of the ability to chew and swallow and the insertion of a gastric feeding tube. While some would simply mourn the loss, Brian accepted this loss by turning it into something humorous. After two nights in the hospital he had composed the "Top Ten Advantages of Having a G-Tube," which he included in his book, in a chapter titled "Laughing and Crying My Way to Heaven":

No. 10   You can brush your teeth while you eat.

No. 9   You can drink all you want and still be able to say "alcohol never touches my lips."

No. 8   You can eat Brussels sprouts and never need to smell them.

No. 7   You can eat at McDonald's and never have to taste the food.

No. 6   You have twice the belly button lint.

No. 5   You can talk with your bag full.

No. 4   You can eat at Hooters and the waitresses stare at you!

No. 3   You never have to complain that the food isn't hot enough.

No. 2   It gives the term "body piercing" a whole new meaning.

No. 1   When you wash out the system you get to drink your own dish water.[20]

Not everyone has Brian's sense of humor, but behind this is a wonderful acceptance of diminishment. It is a subject addressed by the Christian church through its history. There is a vast literature in the European Middle Ages (fifteenth century) on the art of dying called *Ars Moriendi*. In his masterful treatment of this literature, Allen Verhey notes how these self-help books, beautifully illustrated with woodcuts, dealt with the temptations of

---

Jesus at the end, pp. 116-19. See also "Lament," in Verhey, *The Christian Art of Dying*, pp. 313-15.

20. Smith, *Closing Comments*, p. 90.

dying — losing faith, despair, impatience, pride — and how these temptations are matched with the virtues in dying — faith, hope, love, and humility.[21] But Verhey notes that while there is much to commend in this literature, almost completely absent is the hope of the resurrection of the body. It is based on the Greek idea of the immortality of the soul, something which still permeates much of Christian thinking today. "The basis of our hope," Verhey affirms, "is the power of God to raise the dead."[22] Verhey then outlines the many ways in which the church and its practices through the story of Jesus "can support practices of dying well and faithfully caring well for the dying."[23]

But final death is preceded by what Walter Wangerin calls "secondary dyings" or "little deaths," including relationships and dreams.[24] These give us practice in acceptance. Acceptance is not compliance. It does not mean to comply with the inevitable, "You've got to." That is not acceptance but fatalism and resignation. To accept is to submit with one's whole being, surrendering to this stage, this loss, this challenge. There is a difference between compliance and submission, often not appreciated in marriage where women claim to be submitting to their husbands when in reality they are complying. Compliance is a psychological adaptation to pain, as it is easier to go along with it than to speak up, to wrestle with it and to come to a full surrender. But with compliance there is always a sliver of resentment. Not so with submission. Submission is something that is done with the freedom of the will. Jesus is the perfect example of this as he prayed in the garden of Gethsemane that the cup of suffering might pass from him. By the third prayer he submitted, "If it is not possible for this cup to pass, your will be done." So acceptance comes from freedom, not from necessity, and it embraces a situation wholeheartedly. Paul Tournier compares this to a woman who suffers acutely from her celibacy and cannot accept

21. Verhey, *The Christian Art of Dying*, pp. 110-56, 255-94.

22. Verhey, *The Christian Art of Dying*, p. 150.

23. Verhey, *The Christian Art of Dying*, pp. 299, 300-385. See also Craddock, Goldsmith, and Goldsmith, *Speaking of Dying*.

24. Walter Wangerin Jr., *Mourning into Dancing* (Grand Rapids: Zondervan, 1992), pp. 78-126.

it. "I did not choose it at all!" she said. "Nuns choose freely in their vows, but I never have!" In response, Tournier advised her to choose the reality, to live the reality to the full, and "thus to readjust her harmony with herself." In so doing, as with aging and its challenges, we can overcome them by accepting them.[25]

Mia Kafieris, struggling with an advancing cancer, reflects on her experience this way:

> One of the most challenging aspects of preparing to potentially die in my experience was the masses of Christian people who encourage me . . . to keep some normality in my life. This often felt like "do things that people who are not facing death [do] to make you feel less like you are going to die." When I spoke with other patients in oncology we often shared our common frustration. Don't they know that this isn't normal and it's not going back to normal and this has become the new normal? And it's no less valuable or important than their perceived normal. . . . [Why, she continues,] can the Christian community not consider the precious time in which a person prepares to die to be as important as other occasions like an engagement, birth, or graduation.[26]

By undertaking these disciplines we are reaffirming the way God has made us, with hearts that are restless until they rest in God. We are built with a thirst for meaning, and that meaning, which is life with God in the kingdom of God, is not found by excusing ourselves from life but by embracing it. Everything, and especially the experiences of aging, is a pathway and movement toward God. Bearing in mind Søren Kierkegaard's great word, that we must live life forward but understand life backward, we could say something for ourselves, as Paul Tournier has said of himself: "So, it is God who made me grow up even before I knew him. It was he who called me to become a doctor. . . . And now it is he who is leading me along

---

25. Tournier, *Learn to Grow Old*, p. 184.

26. Mia Kafieris, "Preparing for Death" (unpublished paper for Regent College, Vancouver, BC, 2013), p. 3.

the new paths of old age."[27] But there is one more valuable exercise to be undertaken in our senior years.

Reviewing Your Life and Straining for the Next

There is value in looking back and doing the work that needs to be done in assessing where we have been, what we have done, what we have left undone, and unreconciled relationships. Bianchi notes that the history of the *memento mori* (the practice of reflecting on death) goes back to ancient times in both spiritual and secular literature. It is certainly encouraged by the Scriptures that call us to "test yourselves" and "remember" (Gal. 6:4; 2 Cor. 13:5). "Repentance for past failings, forgiveness by God and neighbor, and ultimate reconciliation with nature, fellow humans, and the divine are elements of this perennial process." And the purpose is to "recollect our lives toward greater integration in face of death."[28] Many modern writings are exactly this: for example, Ernest Hemingway's "The Snows of Kilimanjaro," Samuel Beckett's "Krapp's Last Tape," and Tolstoy's *The Death of Ivan Ilyich*. God the Holy Spirit, says Bianchi, is active in this process "to draw good out of the failures of our lives."[29] How to do this?

It can be done in a retreat setting, where a person takes three or four days in solitude to review one's life, writing, praying, reflecting, and worshipping. It can be done sequentially by writing stories of your own life that can be passed on to children and friends, not excluding the hard moments from the text. By processing the hardest experiences of our lives, we can see that they were possibly the best growing and learning times, but it did not feel like that when we experienced them. God is in the business of redemption, and these difficult patches are part of our story. Failures revisited and recontextualized can become ministers of grace to us and others. Frederick Buechner elaborates on this brilliantly:

27. Tournier, *Learn to Grow Old*, p. 214.
28. Bianchi, *Aging as a Spiritual Journey*, pp. 171-72.
29. Bianchi, *Aging as a Spiritual Journey*, pp. 171-72.

My interest in the past is not, I think, primarily nostalgic. Like everybody else, I rejoice in much of it and marvel at those moments when, less by effort than by grace, it comes to life again with extraordinary power and immediacy. But what quickens my pulse now is the stretch ahead rather than the one behind, and it is mainly for some clue to where I am going that I search through where I have been, for some hint as to who I am becoming or failing to become that I delve into what I used to be.[30]

The philosopher Cicero wrote a unique apology for how to achieve and flourish in elderhood in his *De Senectute*. Essentially he proposed sound nutrition, exercise, sensual moderation, an active mental life, and reflection — not bad advice for aging people in the twenty-first century.[31] Why do this? We do this to finish this life well.

Finishing Well

But how can we finish well? Here are some principles.

First, we must keep articulating our life goals, not just when we are young and are starting a new project but all the way along. It is helpful to have a personal mission statement and to keep it before your eyes. Mine is to love God with all my heart; to love and cherish my wife and children through provision, affirmation, and protection; to empower the people of God for service in the world and church; and to beautify God's world by making beautiful things. Dr. Walter Wright asks three questions: (1) What is the most important thing in your life right now? (and do not quickly say "God"); (2) What do you want your life to be about? and (3) At this point in your life, what do you want to learn next?

Second, constantly refresh your sense of calling. Calling helps us finish well with respect to three of life's challenges. (1) It keeps us

30. Quoted in Small, *When Christians Retire*, p. 30. See section on memory and Augustine in Hauerwas, *Growing Old in Christ*, pp. 274ff.

31. Schachter-Shalomi, *From Age-ing to Sage-ing*, p. 62.

journeying purposefully to the very end of our lives.[32] (2) Calling helps to prevent us from confusing the termination of our occupation with the termination of our vocations — the two are not the same.[33] (3) Calling encourages us to leave the entire outcome of our lives to God. In one of the evocative servant songs in the Old Testament book of Isaiah, the servant of the Lord says, "I have labored in vain. I have spent my strength for nothing at all. *Yet what is due me is in the* LORD'*s hand, and my reward is with my God*" (Isa. 49:4, italics mine).

Third, each of us needs to have an accountability group. This is a small group of people who know us well and who are willing to meet with us from time to time to examine what we are doing with our lives, with our thoughts, with our talents, and even with our money. They need to ask about our relationships, especially with spouse, children, and people of the other sex. They need to explore our vulnerabilities and our strengths and to name the lie in us. Yes, it is worth having an accountability group that may ask how much money we are making and what we are doing with it. Who knows how much we earn and what we do with it?

Fourth, if you are married, stay with the wife or husband of your youth. Practice chastity within marriage. And not just by avoiding extramarital sexual affairs, or divorcing to get a newer and younger model. We have to practice chastity in our thought life, pruning our lives of images and influences that encourage sexual promiscuity.

Fifth, practice thanksgiving day and night. The theologian John Calvin said that gratitude is the fundamental spiritual posture of the Christian person. How could this be? Scripture certainly points this way. In Romans 1, Paul explains the essential problem of human beings. They have neither revered God — admitting that they are not themselves God and that God is worthy of reverent affection, usually called "the fear of the Lord" — nor have they been thankful (Rom. 1:21). Gratitude is the recognition that we are not autonomous, that we depend on God for everything, that God is good, that

---

32. Os Guinness, *The Call: Finding and Fulfilling the Central Purpose of Your Life* (Nashville: Word Publishing, 1998), pp. 241-42.

33. Guinness, *The Call*, p. 242.

life is good, and that we are not masters of our own destiny. In an older classic, Francis Schaeffer suggests that one test of the spiritual life is whether we love God enough to be contented. Otherwise we will revolt against God and allow our circumstances, especially the negative and hard ones, to foster a root of bitterness.[34]

Personally, the first time I read the apostle's confession in Philippians 4:11-12 — "I have learned to be content whatever the circumstances. I know what it is to be in need, and I know what it is to have plenty" — I thought to myself, I have surely learned the secret of being discontent. Then I looked carefully at the passage and saw that we can do all things through Christ (v. 13) and that the way of accessing this grace is by "prayer and petition, with thanksgiving" (v. 6). Joan Chittister, in *The Gift of Years,* points out the special role that gratitude plays at this stage of life:

> We have every right to live in gratitude for all the stages of life that brought us here, for all the memories that give us great joy, the people who helped us get this far, the accomplishments we carved on our hearts along the way. These experiences cry out to be celebrated. They are no more past than we are. They live in us forever.[35]

So how do we do this? By bombarding our discontentment with thanksgiving to God — day and night, moment by moment. As we have said earlier, thanksgiving is expected by our Creator. But it also has results: contentment, peace, and joy. A friend who is struggling with cancer is constantly thankful, in particular, recognizing that this is the best time in human history to have the disease, as there are wonderful medical interventions available.

Thanksgiving drives away discontentment, keeps us focused on what God is doing and has done, keeps us from attributing our

---

34. Francis A. Schaeffer, *True Spirituality* (Wheaton, IL: Tyndale House, 1971), p. 9.

35. Joan Chittister, quoted in Lewis Richmond, *Aging as a Spiritual Practice: A Contemplative Guide to Growing Older and Wiser* (New York: Gotham Books, 2012), p. 62.

success to ourselves, and so is an effective antidote to pride. It keeps us from becoming the center of the universe.

Finally, keep our focus not only on this life but also on the life to come. "Life," says Richard Rohr, "is all about practicing for heaven."[36] As Bianchi notes in the quotation above, we need not only life review but also life preview, the subject we considered in the last chapter.

The philosopher George Santayana said, "There is no cure for birth and death save to enjoy the interval."[37] This accurately expresses the practical theology of a generation that denies death, fails to believe in a new heaven and new earth, and therefore is preoccupied with fitness, health, and pleasure. But the Christian approach, as J. I. Packer once said, is to "regard readiness to die as the first step in learning to live."[38] Martin Luther preached a sermon entitled "On the Resurrection" on Easter Sunday 1544, which expresses the hope implicit in this eloquently:

> God will create a new heaven and a new earth, wherein righteousness shall dwell. It will be no arid waste, but a beautiful new earth, where all the just will dwell together. There will be no carnivorous beasts, or venomous creatures, for all such, like ourselves, will be relieved from the curse of sin, and will be to us as friendly as they were to Adam in Paradise. There will be little dogs, with golden hair, shining like precious stones. The foliage of the trees, and the verdure of the grass, will have the brilliancy of emeralds; and we ourselves delivered from our mundane subjection to gross appetites and necessities, shall have the same form as here, but infinitely more perfect. Our eyes shall be radiant as the purest silver, and we shall be exempt from all sickness and tribulation. We shall behold the glorious Creator face to face; and then, what ineffable satisfaction will it be to find our relations and friends among the just![39]

36. Rohr, *Falling Upward*, p. 101.

37. Quoted in T. K. Jones, "Death: Real Meaning in Life Is to Be Found beyond Life," *Christianity Today* 35 (June 24, 1991): 30.

38. Quoted in Jones, "Death," p. 30.

39. *The Table Talk of Martin Luther* (London: H. G. Bohn, 1857), pp. 322-23.

When two of our grandchildren were quite small, they were playing in a small children's tent in our living room. The little girl, about three, said to the boy, about four, "Let's play mommy and daddy." To which he agreed. While holding a doll, they pretended they were bathing a child (with appropriate sounds of swish swish). Then she said, "Let's put the baby down to sleep." And they both sang "Lullaby Baby," in perfect tune. "Now let's us go to bed." And there was silence for a couple of minutes. (My wife was just outside the tent monitoring the situation!) Then our granddaughter said in an acidly cheery voice, "It's morning time. Time to get up!" He grumbled, "It's not morning time. I don't want to get up." To which she repeated the wake-up call, "Time to get up." He protested once more. But then she said, "If you don't get up we can't play." Suddenly he said, "I'm late for work!" "Then," she said, "give me a hug before you go." He said, "I don't have time for a hug" as he left the room.

What were they doing? Playing grown-up life. And that indeed is what we are doing, not only in keeping Sabbath — a foretaste of the threefold rest of God, humankind, and creation — but in all of life and especially as we approach the end. We are playing heaven. The best is yet to be.

Personal or Group Study: Numbering Our Days: Psalm 90

We do not know how long we will live. But we know that on average women live longer than men, and both men and women today in the developed world are living beyond the seventy years mentioned in the psalm and well into their eighties. So what? Using the enigmatic verse in Psalm 90 about "numbering our days" (v. 12), should we take the national average life span and calculate the actual number of days left between now and our eventual demise? Then, having come up with that number, should we figure out a way to make the maximum use of those days? Or should we develop a "bucket list" of things we want to do before we "kick the bucket," that delightful metaphor for our last gasp? Or should we simply live one day at a time as though we were going to live forever, which for Christians is a delightful prospect. Or, knowing that life is short, should we eat, drink, and be merry and squeeze all we can out of this life? A whole generation seems to be doing this, but the idea is not new. The pagan Corinthians, and some of the believers in Corinth, without a resurrection hope, were, the apostle Paul suggests, simply giving themselves to the mantra (quoted from Isaiah) "Let us eat and drink, for tomorrow we die" (1 Cor. 15:32). Psalm 90, technically one of the laments in the Psalter, puts the brevity of our lives into an eternal perspective that is truly invigorating and faith forming.

Personal Reflection:
When have you been tempted to see the brevity of life as leading to the reasonableness of eating and drinking and making merry? When and why?

Group Discussion:
Talk about how your own parents handled and spoke about, if they did, the experience of growing older. What do you think was the source of their perspective?

Read Psalm 90
1. Søren Kierkegaard said that life is lived forward but understood backward. Why do you think the psalmist, here identified as Moses, begins by looking toward the past (vv. 1-2)?
2. What picture does the psalmist give of growing older (vv. 3-11)? Who does he say is responsible for this situation?
3. How do you personally regard your experience of aging? How could this be different if you took the perspective of this psalm?
4. In the Bible wisdom is not mere information but practical know-how on how to live well. Why do you think the psalmist is making a connection between numbering our days and growing wiser (v. 12)?
5. What wisdom do you think can be gained by "numbering our days," if not in hard numbers, at least in recognizing our limited life span on earth? Is it a good thing to form a "bucket list" of things you want to do before you die? If so, why? If not, why not?

6. What is the psalmist's faith and prayer response as he turns to God in his lament about the brevity and difficulty of life (vv. 13-15)?
7. What does the psalmist ask of God about God's own work and his work as a human being (vv. 16-17)?
8. What work of your hands, heart, or head would you pray to God to establish?
9. While this psalm does not offer the Christian hope of resurrection from the dead and life everlasting, what valuable perspective does it bring on the universal experience of aging? Why is this perspective healthier (both emotionally and spiritually) than refusing to acknowledge the difficulty of growing old and eventually dying?

"O God, our help in ages past,
Our hope for years to come,
Our shelter from the stormy blast,
And our eternal home."

Isaac Watts

Now or Later:
Make a different kind of "bucket list" than simply "these are the experiences or travels I want to have before I die." Make a list of the following:

- What values do I want to develop?
- What relationships do I want to develop?
- What do I want to learn?
- What service do I want to develop?

9

The End That Is the Beginning

Death is largely a threat to those who have not yet lived their life.

Richard Rohr[1]

The human being has always lost his way; but now he has lost his address.

G. K. Chesterton[2]

Our culture seems increasingly moving to the view that aging itself is an illness, and if it is possible, we ought to create and fund research that promises that we may be able to get out of life alive.

Stanley Hauerwas[3]

1. Richard Rohr, *Falling Upward: A Spirituality for the Two Halves of Life* (San Francisco: Jossey-Bass, 2011), p. xxxvi.

2. G. K. Chesterton, *What's Wrong with the World*, in *The Collected Works of G. K. Chesterton*, vol. 4 (San Francisco: Ignatius Press, 1987), p. 77, quoted in Gilbert Meilaender, *Should We Live Forever? The Ethical Issues of Aging* (Grand Rapids: Eerdmans, 2013), p. 79.

3. Stanley Hauerwas, "How Risky Is *The Risk of Education*? Random Reflections from the American Context," in *The State of the University* (Malden, MA: Blackwell, 2007), p. 53, quoted in Fred Craddock, Dale Goldsmith, and Joy V. Gold-

I had been working as a carpenter for a few weeks after leaving a thriving university church as pastor in order to plant a church among street people and to reengage the work world of ordinary people. Alongside me was another tradesperson, a drywall taper — the person who tapes and muds the joints between sheets of plaster. We talked during coffee breaks and lunch hours when he munched his moose meat sandwiches and boasted about his latest hunting trip up north. But one day, in all seriousness, he asked, "Paul, what happens to us when we die?" No pastor would have been asked that question because my colleague had never darkened the door of a church. It is a good question, and one we almost dare not ask, especially today.

In my lifetime the fig leaf has slipped twice. That famous fig leaf pictured in traditional paintings of Adam and Eve in the garden of Eden, covering their private parts, no longer covers sex. People can now talk freely about their sexual needs, longings, and experiences. But next the fig leaf has slipped over the wallet or purse. For a long time people could not talk about how much money they were making, what they did with it, and what it meant to them. That too is passing. Now the new unmentionable is death. Not death in general, or someone else's death, but my death.[4]

One of our dear friends was dying. She knew it, and we knew it. Breaking the silence on the subject but surrounded by lifelong friends who were going to sing her into the next life, she said, "I don't know how to die." It is a profound statement. In time another friend (mentioned in the last chapter) passed after keeping a journal for months of progressive illness. I visited along with others weekly, and one day he showed me his journal. I read it and asked if I could edit it and share it with his family and friends when he died. He did give permission and did die, and I did my part by putting his reflections into a published book. Some of his "closing comments" are found in

smith, *Speaking of Dying: Recovering the Church's Voice in the Face of Death* (Grand Rapids: Brazos Press, 2012), p. 33.

4. Some of the following was first published as Gail C. Stevens and R. Paul Stevens, "Death," in Robert Banks and R. Paul Stevens, eds., *The Complete Book of Everyday Christianity* (Downers Grove, IL: InterVarsity Press, 1997), pp. 273-78.

this book. It is a rare exposé on dying in faith, not just living until you die, but dying well.

Death denial, however, does not exist in all cultures, especially where death is not sanitized and quarantined in hospitals. Gail and I served in Africa for parts of ten years; in that continent life expectancy is low and death is a daily event — from car accidents (epidemic), malaria, AIDS, dysentery, and war. The African Brotherhood Church of East Africa is one of the indigenous Christian churches that has emerged without much help or influence from the West. They developed their own hymnody rather than merely translating hymns and songs from the West into the tribal language. I had a student research both the rhythm and the words of these hymns and was shocked to find what these Christians sing about. Eighty percent of the songs were about heaven and the second coming of Jesus — that grand rendezvous at the end of history. It is different in the North and West, even though we have an academic discipline — thanatology — to explore death. As one terminally ill patient put it, "Preparing for death is often lost in wider conversations of ethics, existentialism, theology, and finer points of eschatology. The reality is that rarely does the research from these conversations offer immediate tangible hope, courage, or preparatory guidance for those who are preparing to die."[5]

Is it important to prepare to die while one is living to the hilt? That is one of the ideas we will address in this chapter. Were the Puritans right to say that we can only live well if we are preparing for death? This is much more than "finishing well" in this life, a subject we have already explored. To do this we must ask, What is death? and What is on the other side of death? If what is on the other side is so good, why are the medical and pharmaceutical worlds trying to prolong life as much as possible?

5. Mia Kafieris, "Preparing for Death" (unpublished paper for Regent College, Vancouver, BC, 2013), p. 1.

The Problem with Prolonging Life Indefinitely

Should We Live Forever? is the title of Gilbert Meilaender's book on the ethical ambiguities of aging.[6] He shows how life-prolongation (the current medical emphasis) and age-retardation (the current aesthetic and cultural push) are not the same thing, though they are related. In fact, what is *not* wanted in our society is life prolongation *without* age retardation! But it is not possible. The famous picture of the old person in Ecclesiastes 12 — hobbling along like a grasshopper supported by two canes — leads the professor to conclude that "there is a time to die" (3:2). Mercifully, as Genesis 3:24 shows, God guards the way back to the tree of immortality in Eden to keep Adam and Eve, and their successors, from getting more and more of the same sinful life, forever. The 1993 movie *Groundhog Day* draws viewers into the experience of a television weatherman who endlessly relives the second of February. Meilaender concludes, "To live forever as we live now would not be paradise but a curse."[7] This is expressed in a deliberately sarcastic way by Mark Twain: "Whoever has lived long enough to find out what life is, knows how deep a debt of gratitude we owe to Adam, the first great benefactor of our race. He brought death into the world."[8]

Death is rarely discussed in polite company and has been tragically separated from everyday life. My wife's father died in his own bed surrounded by children, grandchildren, and eight great-grandchildren. We all said our goodbyes and blessed him. It was unusual, I admit. Instead of dying at home surrounded by relatives and friends, we normally die in a hospital surrounded by machines. Death has become institutionalized. In older cultures, before medical science became capable of prolonging life by two or three de-

---

6. Gilbert Meilaender, *Should We Live Forever? The Ethical Ambiguities of Aging* (Grand Rapids: Eerdmans, 2013).

7. Meilaender, *Should We Live Forever?* p. 41.

8. Quoted in "Introduction," Richard John Neuhaus, ed., *The Eternal Pity: Reflections on Dying* (Notre Dame: University of Notre Dame Press, 2000), p. 11. Neuhaus has a magnificent summary of death in various traditions — Buddhist, Islamic, Jewish, and Hindu — drawing on the literature of these religious traditions as well as secular literary works.

cades, people expected death at any time, if not from disease, then from childbirth, famine, plague, or war. These days, people do not expect to die. Few people actually see someone die, except for those in the medical profession, and dying for them is often surrounded by a sense of failure.

Death has also been sanitized. Instead of washing the person's body and digging the grave themselves, something still done in rural Africa, the family arranges for a mortician to prepare the body to be as "lifelike" as possible and displayed for all to see, though rarely in one's home. The funeral service takes place in a mortuary chapel, and the body is delivered hygienically to the flames or the soil. The cemetery is not likely to be found in the courtyard of the family church but in a place apart. It may never, or only rarely, be visited. In contrast, my friend in Kenya walks past his wife's grave mound every time he goes to the maize field of his small farm. To gain a theology and spirituality of death will involve recovering the connection between this once-in-a-lifetime experience and everyday living. To do that, we must also try to understand just what death is.

What Is Death Anyway?

Both the Old and New Testaments say much about death. In his brilliant study of Old Testament anthropology, Hans Walter Wolff explores in detail several dimensions of death and dying.[9] Critical to the Old Testament narrative is that the Israelites approached death, dying, and the grave different from the surrounding nations. The dead were not to be consulted through witchcraft. Graves were not to be worshipped. Death was not to be mythologized into a religious thing. "No holiness whatever, let alone divinity, consecrates death, any more than the grave."[10] There was to be no cult of the dead. While Israel's neighbors would cut their bodies when someone

---

9. The words of the dying, the grave, the demythologizing of death, Yahweh and the vacuum of death, stages of dying, the death of the one and the death of the many. Hans Walter Wolff, *Anthropology of the Old Testament* (Philadelphia: Fortress Press, 1974), pp. 99-118.

10. Wolff, *Anthropology*, p. 102.

had died, presumably to make the mourners unrecognizable and undiscoverable to the dead, "such respect for death is impossible in Yahweh's presence."[11] But one who has died has been cut off from praise of God's works and word. "In the Old Testament life there means: to have relationship, above all, to have relationship with God. Death means lack of relationship."[12]

Yet even in the Old Testament, God is not absent from the world of the dead. "If I make my bed in the depths, you are there" (Ps. 139:8). Wolff concludes, "Life cannot end in death for the man for whom God himself has become the subsistence of life."[13] Even in the Old Testament, God overcomes death. In the New Testament, building on the resurrection of Jesus, we discover new dimensions of how God overcomes death. First, nothing, not even death, can separate us from the love of God in Jesus Christ (Rom. 8:38-39). Second, death becomes the gateway to an even better life ultimately in the new heaven and new earth of which this life, sown into the ground, is like a seed compared with a full-grown plant (1 Cor. 15:35-58). Yet there is a mystery in death revealed in the word describing Jesus' death on the cross, namely, that he "gave up his spirit" (Luke 23:46).

My father died of pneumonia in my brother's arms after being unable to speak or eat for two years. He was not afraid to die, but he seemed to be lingering, hanging on, for reasons we could not discover. His wife, my mother, had died months before, and there was no unfinished business known to us or admitted by him. My brother embraced him and said, "Dad, it's all right to go." And within minutes he died peacefully, sleeping in Jesus. But he left us wondering about the mystery of death, its timing, its meaning, and the strange way that we are created by God to hang on to life, sometimes even longer than we need. It is difficult to tell yourself to die, but do we have some part in giving up our spirits? An important question in this matter is: When is someone dead?

Clinically *death* is defined as the cessation of heartbeat,

---

11. Wolff, *Anthropology*, p. 105.
12. Wolff, *Anthropology*, pp. 106-7.
13. Wolff, *Anthropology*, p. 109.

breathing, and brain activity. At this point a physician pronounces someone "dead." Yet it is widely recognized that a person as a fully robed body-soul-spirit being may have died hours and perhaps even months earlier. The ambiguity of the matter is highlighted by the intrusion of technology. Life can be artificially prolonged on machines, sometimes with the purpose of "harvesting" organs for transplants from a dead-yet-still-living being who will die, in all respects, once the machines are turned off. Or will he or she? Does the soul remain near for a while to be reunited should the person be resuscitated by starting the heart and breathing again? There are documented stories of near-death experiences or "coming back from the other side" experiences. Did the person actually die when brain activity ceased, perhaps in a traumatic car accident, even though clinically the person remained living? Is it possible to die months before clinical death by becoming incapable of giving and receiving love, perhaps through a debilitating disease that puts the person in a "vegetative" state? If so, there are many walking dead in this world. Such is the ambiguity of the subject.

There were two trees in the garden of Eden: the tree of life (presumably offering immortality [Gen. 2:9]) and the tree offering godlike knowledge of good and evil. Adam and Eve could live forever only if they accepted their creaturely limitations, eating from the first tree and refusing to eat from the second, the autonomy tree. If they took from the knowledge tree, they would die (3:3). But there were dimensions of that death other than simply returning to the dust (3:19). They died to oneness with God (spiritual death), intimacy with each other (relational death), and trusteeship of the world (vocational death).

Would Adam and Eve, if they had not sinned, have died of old age, perhaps in a transition like Enoch's that led to fuller life with God? We do not know. Significantly, the first death in the narrative was not God-inflicted but brought by humankind on itself: the murder of Abel. Equally significant is the growing consciousness of sin-cursed death by the characters of the drama exemplified in Cain's plea for protection from a violent death (4:14-15) and Eve's plea for a replacement son to fill the emptiness left by death (4:25). So whatever might have been possible in Paradise before human sin, death has become something terrible, something fraught with spiritual consequences, something to be feared. It is more than mere physical annihilation.

Death of the Whole Person

The author of Hebrews says that Jesus tasted death for everyone (Heb. 2:9), clearly indicating that whatever death has become through sin — in all its psychological and spiritual consequences (Matt. 27:46) — was experienced by Jesus on the cross. Death is more than the mere stopping of the heart, breathing, and brain activity.

Understood biblically, persons are not souls with bodily wrappings but ensouled bodies or embodied souls, a psycho-pneuma-somatic unity. The body does not "contain" a soul to be released through death — a fundamentally Greek notion that has permeated European culture. The body is the expressiveness of soul and the soul the heart of body. But these are so interdependently connected, indeed interfused, that to touch either is to touch both — hence the seriousness of sexual sin. We do not "have" bodies and "have" souls but *are* bodies and souls. So death, to the Hebrew mind, cannot strike the body without striking the soul, a connection that is not clear in many English translations that substitute "person" for "soul" or "body."[14] For example, "the soul that doeth aught presumptuously . . . shall be cut off from the people" (Num. 15:30 KJV) contrasts with the newer Today's New International Version translation: "But anyone who sins defiantly . . . must be cut off from their people." However much we may qualify this in the light of passages like "today you will be with me in paradise" (Luke 23:43), we must still deal with death as death *of a person,* not just of a person's shell.[15]

More than our bodies die: emotions, personality, capacity for

---

14. J. Pedersen, *Israel: Its Life and Culture,* 4 vols. (London: Geoffrey Cumberlege, 1964), 1:179.

15. For a contrary view, see J. W. Cooper, *Body, Soul, and Life Everlasting: Biblical Anthropology and the Monism-Dualism Debate* (Grand Rapids: Eerdmans, 1989).

relationships, capacity for giving and receiving love. Do our spirits die or at least "taste" death? We simply do not know whether we enter into a "soul sleep" until the day of resurrection or persist in some kind of "intermediate state," as it is called in theological texts, until Christ comes again and the dead are raised. What we do know is that death is more than a merely physical phenomenon. The whole person dies. We are obviously dealing with a mystery, but it is a mystery with windows.

A Vanquished Power

In all this we admit that we are facing a formidable power. Death holds people in slavery to lifelong fear (Heb. 2:15). The fear may have multiple sources: fear of pain, of the unknown, of having to experience something we cannot control or predict, of losing all that is familiar and dear to us. Many older people fear increasing withering, loss of dignity, and loss of independence, all preludes to death. A profound fear we carry from our earliest infancy is the fear of being dropped; the fear of death is the anxiety that when we can no longer hang on, we will be dropped and plunge into nothingness. Deeper still is the fear of unpredictable consequences after the grave if there is a God. We are ultimately accountable to God, and the happy continuation into the "next" life is contingent on what we do in this life. Death is fraught with eternal consequences. But nothing, not even rebellion or suicide, can "separate us from the love of God which is in Christ Jesus our Lord" (Rom. 8:39).

The fact that human beings cannot simply treat death as a way of recycling people illustrates what Scripture proclaims: death is one of the principalities and powers. Paul spoke of death as the last enemy (Rom. 8:38; 1 Cor. 15:26) because it seems death has a "life of its own," making its pretentious claims on human hearts and holding them captive to their mortality. This last enemy was destroyed by the death of Christ, this death of death being certified by the resurrection of Christ. For the person found in Christ, death is not fraught with temporal fear or eternal consequences, as it is for those who have heard the gospel and rejected relationship with God. Yet we still must die. Scripture speaks of death as a great sleep,[16] as a returning to dust,[17] as a departure,[18] as a blissful reunion,[19] and as a coming face-to-face with Christ.[20] But what we want to know is what it is like on the other side. N. T. Wright calls this "life after life after death." There are four dimensions to this: resurrection, renewal, rendezvous, and rest.

Life after Life after Death

First, there is the resurrection of persons. We are not told when or how. Is this at the end of history, and if so, will we be in some kind of soul sleep until the end if we die before the consummation of all human history? We have no definitive answer to this question except that when we die we are with the Lord.[21] But the great invigorating future promised for those in Christ is not the immortality of the soul — a Greek idea — but the resurrection of the body. As we have discussed, we are ensouled bodies or embodied souls, whole persons with a dimension of longing for God and heaven (our soulish selves). While Jewish people cherished this hope before the time of Jesus, we now have certain proof and a practical demonstration of this future right on this planet.

The epicenter of our hope for life through death is the resurrection of Jesus. Only one person has come back from the dead to tell us about the other side. The Gospels record all we need to know about Jesus after his death: (1) he had a real body that could walk, cook, eat, and speak — this was no mere phantom or angelic presence; (2) there is a continuity between the body in this life and the body in the next, so much so that the disciples recognized him — a powerful hint that we may recognize one another in the New Jeru-

---

16. Dan. 12:2; Job 3:17; 1 Thess. 4:14; Rev. 14:13.

17. Gen. 3:19-22; Eccles. 12:7; Rom. 5:12.

18. Luke 9:31; 16:22; Acts 9:39; Phil. 1:23; 2 Pet. 1:15; James 2:26.

19. Gen. 25:8; Judg. 2:10.

20. Luke 23:43; 2 Cor. 5:8; Phil. 1:23.

21. See an excellent treatment of this issue in Allen Verhey, *The Christian Art of Dying: Learning from Jesus* (Grand Rapids: Eerdmans, 2011), pp. 203-7.

salem; (3) there were continuing evidences of things experienced in bodily life in this world, namely, the scars; and (4) the scars were not now the marks of sin but a means of grace, as Jesus invited Thomas to touch and believe.

From the resurrection of Jesus we are able to say that there is both discontinuity and continuity between this life and the next. The apostle Paul calls our postresurrection body a "spiritual body," meaning that we are not shapeless spirits floating in the ether of heaven but truly embodied people in a form that is completely expressive of our spiritual or soulish longings and desires. Paul makes the comparison between a seed and a mature plant. If we are to be truly human, more human than we have ever been in this life, we shall enjoy relationship, creativity, enterprise, work, and above all the beautiful presence of God. Many people cram into this short life on earth everything they could possibly get and experience, as though there is nothing more, which there is.

The fourth-century church father St. Augustine's defense of the resurrection of the body "includes how the aged will be raised but he is more concerned with other questions: How can an earthly body exist in heaven? Will abortions be raised? What about our hair and nail clippings? What about cannibalism? His key text is Ephesians 4:13: 'until we all attain . . . the stature of the full maturity of Christ.'" Thus, concludes Augustine, "Each person will be given the stature which he had in his prime, even though he was an old man when he died, or, if he died before maturity, the stature he would have attained. . . . [I]f the words [of Eph. 4:13] refer to bodily resurrection, we must take them to mean that the bodies of the dead will rise neither younger nor older than Christ. They will be the same age, the same prime of life, which Christ, as we know had reached."[22] It is a nice thought, whether conjectural or prophetic, but it does affirm what Scripture does, namely, that we will be better!

Christian hope promises a renewal, not a replacement. Our bodies, souls, and spirits are transfigured and "will be like his

22. Rowan A. Greer, "Special Gift and Special Burden: Views of Old Age in the Early Church," in Stanley Hauerwas et al., eds., *Growing Old in Christ* (Grand Rapids: Eerdmans, 2003), p. 25.

[Christ's] glorious body" (Phil. 3:21). But it is not just human beings that will be renewed.

Second, there is the coming renewal of everything. Years ago Lesslie Newbigin said that as a generation we are "without conviction about any worthwhile end to which the travail of history might lead."[23] But the truth is this: the world will not end with a bang or a fizzle but with the glorious coming of Jesus and the renewal of everything, even the scars we have made on the planet. Contrary to what is taught and believed by so many North American Christians, that this world is going up in smoke, the end is not the annihilation of creation and then the miraculous creation of a new world and new heaven out of nothing. Rather it is the renewal, the transfiguration, of everything. The image of 2 Peter is not the reduction of everything to its elements and then the snuffing out of everything, in anticipation of a brand-new new creation. Rather the image is one of putting rough ore into a hot cauldron and then turning up the heat to burn out the dross — this being quite probably the meaning in 2 Peter 3:10. This makes an enormous difference to how we view our work in this world and our stewardship of creation.

In other words, our works done in this life are transfigured rather than annihilated. Even the creation itself will not be annihilated but transfigured. The prophet Ezekiel envisions the land "radiant" with the glory of God (Ezek. 43:2), a prophetic announcement that the earth will become "a new earth" (Rev. 21:1), just as the psychological body (literally, "natural" in the Greek) will be transfigured into a "spiritual body" (1 Cor. 15:44). In other words, the Christian hope is not the survival of the spirit after the death of the body or even the continuation of an immortal (but disembodied) soul in a nonmaterial "heaven" or the provision of another body, soul, and spirit to be given us through reincarnation. The hope is both material and spiritual — not just a "new" body but a renewed body, not just a new earth but a renewed earth.

Heaven comes to earth, or in reality there will be a final and full merging of heaven and earth — the invisible and the visible.

---

23. Lesslie Newbigin, *Honest Religion for Secular Man* (Philadelphia: Westminster Press, 1966), p. 42.

We too easily drop "new earth" from a "new heaven and new earth."
Yves Congar is the theologian who did much of the preparatory
work in advance of Vatican II. In his *Lay People in the Church* he
says: "Ontologically, this is the world that, transformed and renewed
will pass into the kingdom; so . . . the dualist position is wrong;
final salvation will be achieved by a wonderful refloating of our
earthly vessel rather than the transfer of the survivors to another
ship wholly built by God."[24] But all this happens at what we can call
the greatest meeting ever — the second coming of Jesus.

Third, there is a grand rendezvous. Hardly anyone hears about
the second coming of Jesus these days except in rural Africa and
some fringe groups that despair of life now and live solidly "in the
future." But the certain coming again of Jesus is one of the inspir-
ing realities for everyday life. William Wilberforce, who is almost
single-handedly responsible for abolishing the slave trade in England, said there was hardly a day when this certain future did not
inspire his mind and action. Scripture is definite about this, not
only in the promise of Jesus to come back as reported in the Gospels
but also in the letters of Paul. First Thessalonians 4:16-18 is worth
quoting at length, partly because it is so easily misunderstood.

> For the Lord himself will come down from heaven, with a loud
> command, with the voice of the archangel and with the trumpet
> call of God, and the dead in Christ will rise first. After that, we
> who are still alive and are left will be caught up together with
> them in the clouds to meet the Lord in the air. And so we will
> be with the Lord forever. Therefore encourage one another with
> these words.

This much we know about the Lord's second coming: it will be a
coming in glory; it will be a universal experience, from the east to the
west; while we do not know when (and we are to remain ready at any
time), there will be no disadvantage for those who have died before
this glorious event; people who mumble that there is "peace and

---

24. Yves Congar, *Lay People in the Church: A Study for a Theology of the Laity,*
trans. D. Attwater (Westminster, MD: Newman Press, 1967), p. 92.

security" (1 Thess. 5:3) will be in for a sudden awakening. God's new world will "break in shining the light of divine judgment and mercy into the world's dark corners," as N. T. Wright says.[25] There will be a grand reunion of believers with the Lord. It is this last point which has stimulated the most imaginative and unhelpful conjecture.

Wright's comments on this are most helpful. He notes how Paul is drawing on Old Testament imagery — the trumpet calls and cosmic events — to describe the importance of the coming of Jesus. He then notes how the language of Jesus "descending" from heaven is metaphorical and does not necessarily mean that heaven is another location within our space but rather is another dimension. Elsewhere Paul uses the language of "appearing" (Col. 3:4) from hiddenness to visibility. Wright continues by addressing himself to the notion that people will find themselves "snatched out of homes, jobs, cars and aeroplanes, leaving the rest of humankind suddenly bereft." Wright shows that this does not mean some "disembodied life in some mid-air 'heaven,' but the re-embodiment of God's people to live with and for God in the new, redeemed world that God will make."[26] This is the grandest rendezvous of all time and then forever. But one other image for the future is that of rest. "There remains, then, a Sabbath-rest for the people of God" (Heb. 4:9).

Fourth, there is vigorous and creative rest. Augustine's much-quoted line, "You [God] have made us for yourself, and our hearts find no rest until they rest in you," is followed by the question, "Who will enable me to find rest in you? Who will grant me that you come to my heart and intoxicate it, so that I forget my evils and embrace my one and only good, yourself?"[27] This great insight applies not only to eternal but also to temporal rest.[28] After we die, what then? An eternity singing the same worship song? As one jaundiced theologian has said, "Heaven did not seem to me worth

25. Tom Wright, *Paul for Everyone: Galatians and Thessalonians* (London: SPCK, 2002), p. 128.

26. Wright, *Paul for Everyone: Galatians and Thessalonians*, pp. 124-25.

27. Augustine, *Confessions*, trans. Henry Chadwick (Oxford: Oxford University Press, 1998), pp. 3, 5.

28. Much of this is drawn from R. Paul Stevens, "Rest," in Banks and Stevens, *The Complete Book of Everyday Christianity*, pp. 853-54.

going to."[29] But just the reverse. The new heaven and new earth is not just worship and work in an amazing community and transformed creation, it is also fantastic rest.

Certainly no one in Christian history has expounded the "rest" that remains for the people of God better than the Puritan Richard Baxter in *The Saints' Everlasting Rest,* which he wrote in 1650. He had been unwell for many days with profuse bleeding and thought he would die shortly. So he began to write and meditate on his heavenly rest. "Being in my quarters, far from home, cast into extreme languishing by the sudden loss of about a gallon of blood . . . I bent my thoughts on my Everlasting Rest; and . . . began to draw up my own funeral sermon, or some helps for my own meditations of heaven, to sweeten both the rest of my life and my death."[30] This book was wildly popular and went through several editions even though it was 844 pages in length. Drawing only on Scripture and with the help of a concordance, Baxter outlined the nature of the everlasting rest that awaits us:

- It is a rest of fulfillment of our faith journey. "There will be no more prayer, because no more necessity, but the full enjoyment of what we prayed for. . . . Preaching is done, the ministry of men ceaseth, sacraments useless. . . ."[31]
- It is a rest of freedom from all evils. "Doubtless there is not such a thing as a pale face, a languid body, feeble joints, unable infancy, decrepit age, peccant humours, dolorous sickness, griping fears, consuming cares or whatsoever deserves the name of evil."[32]
- It is a rest of personal perfection. "Here eye hath not seen, nor ear heard, nor heart conceived what God hath laid up for them that wait for him."[33]

29. R. Paul Stevens, "Boredom," in Banks and Stevens, *The Complete Book of Everyday Christianity,* p. 80.

30. Richard Baxter, *The Saints' Everlasting Rest,* ed. John T. Wilkinson (Vancouver: Regent College Publishing, 2004), p. 23.

31. Baxter, *The Saints' Everlasting Rest,* pp. 38-39.

32. Baxter, *The Saints' Everlasting Rest,* p. 39.

33. Baxter, *The Saints' Everlasting Rest,* p. 39.

- It is a rest of knowing and enjoying God fully. "If the Lord lift up the light of his countenance on us here, it puts more gladness in our hearts than the world's increase can do. How much more when in his light we shall have light without darkness and he shall make us full of joy with his countenance."[34]
- It is the rest of both body and soul being perfected. "As much as a body spiritual, above the sun in glory, exceedeth these frail, noisome, diseased, lumps of flesh or dirt, that now carry about us; so far shall our sense of seeing and hearing exceed these we now possess."[35]
- It is a rest in which we experience the fulfillment of love and joy. "Thou shalt be eternally embraced in the arms of that love, which was from everlasting, and will extend to everlasting; of that love which brought the Son of God's love from heaven to earth, from earth to the cross, from the cross to the grave, from the grave to glory; that love which was weary, hungry, tempted, scorned, scourged, buffeted, spit upon, crucified, pierced; which did fast, pray, teach, heal, weep, sweat, bleed, die — that love will eternally embrace thee."[36]
- It is a rest in which we enjoy the fellowship of the blessed saints and angels of God. It will be a "corporation of perfected saints, whereof Christ is the head; the communion of saints completed."[37]
- It is a perfect rest from suffering, "from our perplexing doubts and fears . . . from all the temptations of Satan . . . from all the abuses and persecutions which we suffer at the hands of wicked men . . . from our sad divisions, and unchristian quarrels with one another . . . from all our personal sufferings, whether natural or ordinary, or extraordinary . . . from all those sad affections which necessarily accompany our absence from God."[38]

I have called this a "vigorous and creative rest." Why? Because we will, in the completion and renewal of everything, be working. As

34. Baxter, *The Saints' Everlasting Rest*, p. 41.
35. Baxter, *The Saints' Everlasting Rest*, p. 42.
36. Baxter, *The Saints' Everlasting Rest*, p. 45.
37. Baxter, *The Saints' Everlasting Rest*, p. 65.
38. Baxter, *The Saints' Everlasting Rest*, pp. 75-82.

we have already seen, we are supposed to work until we die, but will we work in the next life? I believe there are strong biblical reasons to suggest this, though the work will be without sweaty and stressful toil and there will be no curse. The principalities and powers, those invisible spiritual, social, and structural forces that make work in this world complicated and just plain hard, will, according to the New Testament, be all brought into complete submission to God (1 Cor. 15:24). The eschatological vision in the Old Testament is that of a humanity at work (Amos 9:13; Mic. 4:3ff.; Isa. 11:1-9; Hos. 2:18-23). This picture is completed for us in the New Testament. The redeemed community will inhabit this new creation in their glorified bodies (1 Cor. 15; Phil. 3:21). They will bring their cultures (Rev. 21:24, 26) and their ethnic and linguistic diversities as well as their gifts (Rev. 5:9).

All this strongly suggests that there will be continuity with our present existence which will undergo a dramatic, transformative, and cathartic renewal. In some way we do not fully understand, our human work and labor will surely find a way into the new creation (Rev. 14:13). It is not just our spiritual work and our spiritual life that will endure and that matter to God, but all work and life undertaken with faith, hope, and love (1 Cor. 13:13; 1 Thess. 1:2-3). The kings of the earth bring their glories into the holy city (Rev. 21:24), and that transfigured creation will be embellished by the deeds of Christians, deeds that "follow them" (Rev. 14:13). So our labor in the lord is "not in vain" (1 Cor. 15:58).

This is good news. In the new heaven and new earth we will be fully human beings who, along with continuous worship, amazing relationships, and awesome experience, will enjoy work as we never did in this life. Hidden talents will be expressed. Creativity that was on the "back burner" for much of our earthly work life will find expression, and our unique and particular giftedness will find expression in a community of giving and receiving, in a form of exchange which, as some have imaginatively suggested, would be business without the passing of money.[39] The last book of the Bible pictures the people of God in these words: "They will rule

---

39. See George MacDonald, *The Curate's Awakening* (Minneapolis: Bethany House, 1985), p. 145.

[read 'work'] with [Christ] age after age after age" (Rev. 22:5).[40] In a profound sense the work we do in this life is preparation for work we will do forever, even if there is no direct correspondence with the actual deed, substance, or subject of our daily work. The giftedness we bring to work, the way we actually work, and, most important of all, for Whom we work will all carry over into the finest workplace in the universe with the best working conditions imaginable.

"In the Lord your labor is not in vain. You are following Jesus and shaping our world in the power of the Spirit; and when the final consummation comes, the work that you have done, whether in Bible study or biochemistry, whether in preaching or in pure mathematics, whether in digging ditches or in composing symphonies, will stand, will last (1 Cor. 15:58)."

N. T. Wright[41]

"Now I lay me down to sleep, I pray thee Lord my soul to keep; if I should die before I wake, I pray thee Lord my soul to take."

A child's prayer, from the twelfth-century *Enchiridion Leonis*[42]

Personal or Group Study: The Life Everlasting: 1 Corinthians 15:12-58; Revelation 7:13-17

Personal Reflection:
With what views of the afterlife did you grow up in your family? Where did these come from?

40. Eugene H. Peterson, *The Message* (Colorado Springs: NavPress, 2002), p. 2264.

41. N. T. Wright, *The Challenge of Jesus: Rediscovering Who Jesus Was and Is* (Downers Grove, IL: InterVarsity Press, 1999), pp. 180-81.

42. Quoted in Richard John Neuhaus, "Introduction," in *The Eternal Pity: Reflections on Dying* (Notre Dame: University of Notre Dame Press, 2000), p. 2.

Group Discussion:

Do you view life prolongation as a good thing? Why? Do you see age retardation as a good thing? Why?

Read 1 Corinthians 15:12-58

1. Why do you think Paul grounds the Christian hope in the physical resurrection of Christ (vv. 12-19)?

2. What difference would it make if Christ had merely survived spiritually, as some today teach, while his body was stolen or displaced (v. 20)?

3. It is often noted that the Christian hope is the resurrection of the body rather than the immortality of the soul, a Greek idea. What difference does it make?

4. What is your own view of your future life after death?

5. How does Paul describe the renewal of everything, even the physical creation (vv. 23-28)? Why is this better than a merely "spiritual heaven" as our final destiny?

6. Paul says that if the dead are not raised, people should simply get as much pleasure out of this short life as possible (vv. 32-34). How do you see this happening in the world today? How does this temptation affect you? Why does Paul call this a sin (v. 34)?

7. In verses 35-49 Paul attempts to describe the indescribable — the continuity we will have with our present bodies and the discontinuity with life now. Trace his argument and the illustrations he uses to make it understandable.

8. Why does Paul insist that the survival of our souls (that inward responsiveness to God) is not enough (v. 50)?

9. Paul argues that what we have done in this life as work in the Lord and of the Lord (not restricting this to stated Christian ministry) will last (v. 58). How will this help us "stand firm" and "be unmoved" (v. 58)?

10. What work of yours can you imagine, work done with faith, hope, and love, may be transformed and find its place in the new heaven and new earth?

Read Revelation 7:13-17

11. Describe the grand rendezvous believers will have in the new heaven and new earth. What will be our experience? What work will we do? What will it be like to be with Jesus? How is this different from a picture of heaven as a place where we play harps and sing the same worship song a million times?

12. How does the life everlasting make a difference to how you will live now?

My friend Angus Gunn wrote a letter before he died to be read afterward:

> I have left this earthly home, not by choice but because I am part of the normal cycle of life. For me it's been a longer cycle than most of my fellow humans enjoyed and I am grateful for every minute of it. At Christmas time in 1947 at age 27 I surrendered my life with all its dreams and hopes to Jesus Christ as my Lord and savior. Out of that relationship came many delights through all the years to follow. I never looked back. Interests broadened and I saw myself as a citizen of the world. Thirteen years after 1947, when I first met Ruth, I discovered that she too had committed her life to Christ in 1947, also at Christmastime, in Pennsylvania. Because consciousness of time disappears at death, I am now in the reality of the new humanity that Jesus won for me through his death and resurrection. The transition was tearful because I had to leave the ones I love dearly and who gave me so very much for so long. I do not know very much about the new humanity. I will not be mortal and I will retain and enjoy within it all that I learned on earth of the person of Jesus, of his love and purpose. I will also discover anew, as I never could on earth, the immensity of that purpose. I think a lot about those I must leave behind. People say that it is what you leave after you are gone that matters. Well, fortunately, our two wonderful children, Heather and Angus Jr., now with their families, far exceed anything that Ruth and I ever imagined we could bequeath to this world.

Epilogue: A Reflection at the Graveside

My friend Brian Smith, mentioned earlier, died of ALS. I had the privilege of editing and publishing his journals of his final years and months under the title *Closing Comments*. His brother Graeme, who was also my former business partner, spoke these words at Brian's graveside. They are a fitting summary of the contents of my own book.

Several years ago at one of several funerals I attended over a relatively short period of time, it occurred to me during the eulogy that there was something inherently false about celebrating a loved one's entrance into eternity solely in terms of praise and commendation and ignoring the half of the whole person that we knew, whose less than admirable characteristics we endured, reproached or suffered; the half of the person for which presumably eternity really meant a sunrise-promised healing and release. I remember sharing this with Brian and he, as usual, instantly understood what I was struggling to give words to, and we talked about it at some length. We ultimately concluded that whatever merits my insight had it would take a very deft touch indeed to pull it off in a funeral without coming off as mean and ill-spirited. I certainly lack that touch, but I do want to attempt to share with you something of my perception of who Brian was as a whole person, and at the same time, share with you what I feel I can say, with some confidence, two brothers think awaits us at the crossroad of life and death and time and eternity.

Over the past few weeks I have thought a lot about the nature of my relationship with my brother. "Close" was the first word that came to mind. But my ready answer prompted me to ask myself how I would define "close." Over the past forty plus years of our adult life I could count on one hand the number of times he and I had done anything together as brothers. We did have an unusually common mind on almost anything we ever talked about when we did get together, but what I think more than anything defined our closeness was our shared conviction that we were failures.

Now, nobody who knew Brian would call him a failure. When five or six hundred people show up at your funeral, you must have been remarkably successful at something! But how others view us and how we view ourselves are two quite separate things. What we imagine others think of us and what they actually do think of us are equally sure to be quite different. And these differences are almost certain to break along all kinds of complex and even contradictory lines. At the root of this phenomenon is what Christian theology defines as original sin, but since that is a concept that is commonly misunderstood (and we have no time here to try to clarify it) I will attempt to describe this root problem in terms of the "broken self."

From the very beginning, our emerging self-consciousness is characterized by brokenness. The conflict between what we want and what our parents want begins in infancy — and that battle waged on the emotional field of desire for parental approval produces the broken self. As we grow older this self-image becomes increasingly complex. Awareness of physical shortcomings, emotional inadequacies, intellectual deficiencies, and habits and character flaws that seem to have genetic inevitability and permanence all contribute to the makeup of our broken selves. Perhaps equally important, the inadequacies and failures of parents, siblings, and others who made up our childhood environment have their own inevitable destructive impact on us. And we live out our lives making strenuous, but largely ineffectual, efforts to compensate for or to conceal this flawed self-image either from ourselves or others. We all struggle with this to varying degrees of success. The few who appear to be unencumbered with such feelings of inadequacy more or less comprise those who "make history" in small ways and large. At the other end are those who are paralyzed by their brokenness and spend their days dumpster-diving and pushing shopping carts full of our refuse. The vast majority of us, however, muddle along as best we can, accompanied by our light and dark angels of hope and despair. Brian was one of us.

My brother as you all know was a very funny guy, but you might not have been aware that his wry, ironic, sometimes even sardonic sense of humor had its roots in his own experiences of frustration and failure. I think at heart he was a clown in the tradition of the legendary Emmett Kelly, the circus clown with the sad face making children laugh. There was often something in Brian's comic performances which transcended the laughter and touched something sadder and much deeper in our experiences together as human beings, that exposed the struggle of our broken selves. His Crash Test Dummies concert stage-crashing performance took place during the final tortuous weeks of Barbara Jean's life when he confessed to me that his sense of inadequacy, confusion, and fear threatened to overwhelm him and he felt he had to do something to break the spell of despair, and what better way to do that than to don the Superman persona. Somehow the staged irony of the Superman cape and his own sense of helplessness in the face of his impending loss was a form of therapy for his soul that must have put a smile on the face of God himself, who I am sure understood it better than Brian did.

I was not present for that appearance of Superman, but I was present for another appearance that will remain indelibly imprinted on my memory more for what it represented than for the comic moment itself. When Brian appeared at his sixtieth birthday party in his Superman costume and his electric wheel chair, it struck me that there could have been no better metaphor than that for his whole life. The lifelong handicap of his inborn pessimism and sense of failure never thwarted his attempts "to leap tall buildings in a single bound." His spirit always longed to be "up, up, and away!" and I think in his illness the more his body mocked him the more his spirit soared. Now of course his Master has taken him "up, up, and away" to a whole other realm!

Had Brian only his humor to aid him in his struggle with the broken self, he would never have become the man we have honored these past two days. As a follower of Jesus he had within reach and touch the ultimate antidote for the broken self — the unconditional love of Jesus.

I don't know about each of you who follow Jesus, but I have found, and I know this was true for Brian, that the efficacy of that divine love is fleeting. We only grasp enough of it to sustain the conviction that it is real and reinforce the hope that one day we'll experience its full resurrection power. There are many who make bold statements about how we can realize it in the here and now, but ironically these promises are usually accompanied by "conditions." I think in the end, it is Jesus who reaches out and grants us those moments of release and freedom; but the reasons and timing are known only to Him.

On the morning of Brian's death, shortly after the undertakers had taken his body away, I sat between Lynn and Craig, and Craig mused about what his father was doing at that moment. Lynn quickly responded that he was breathing deeply and freely, inhaling and exhaling without encumbrance. In these reflective moments the dominant feeling I am experiencing is not grief but rather envy. Now finally my brother can breathe, without hindrance, the divine air of unconditional love. When the Lord of the Universe, face to face, cast those eyes of love on Brian, the spell of his broken self was broken forever, and now he is soaring in ways we can't even dream of.[1]

---

1. Brian A. Smith, *Closing Comments: ALS — a Spiritual Journey into the Heart of a Fatal Affliction* (Toronto: Clements Publishing, 2000), pp. 134-38.

Bibliography

(* = especially recommended)

1. General

Arn, Win, and Charles Arn. *Catch the Age Wave: A Handbook for Effective Ministry with Senior Adults.* Kansas City, MO.: Beacon Hill Press, 1999.

Arnold, Johann Christoph. *Rich in Years: Finding Peace and Purpose in a Long Life.* Walden, NY: The Plough Publishing House, 2013.

*Bianchi, Eugene. *Aging as a Spiritual Journey.* New York: Crossroad, 1984. Highly recommended book especially on elderhood.

Bolles, Richard. *The Three Boxes of Life: And How to Get Out of Them.* Berkeley, CA: Ten Speed Press, 1981. Explores the wisdom of continuing study, work, and play throughout life.

Borrie, Cathie. *The Long Hello.* New York: Simon & Schuster, 2015.

Buford, Bob. *Half Time: Changing Your Game Plan from Success to Significance.* Grand Rapids: Zondervan, 1994. As the subtitle suggests, this book explores mid-life transition.

Diehl, William E., and Judith R. Diehl. *It Ain't Over Till It's Over: A User's Guide to the Second Half of Life.* Minneapolis: Augsburg Books, 2003. A very practical guide on many aspects of retirement.

Fischer, Kathleen. *Winter Grace: Spirituality for Later Years.* Mahwah, NJ: Paulist Press, 1985.

Griffin, Emilie. *Souls in Full Sail: A Christian Spirituality for the Later Years.* Downers Grove, IL: InterVarsity Press, 2011.

Hanson, Amy. *Baby Boomers: Tapping the Ministry Talents and Passions of Adults over 50*. A Leadership Network Publication. San Francisco: Jossey-Bass, 2010.

*Houston, James. *The Mentored Life: From Individualism to Personhood*. Colorado Springs: NavPress, 2002. A substantive reflection on spiritual aspects of relationality.

*Houston, James M., and Michael Parker. *A Vision for the Aging Church: Renewing Ministry for and by Seniors*. Downers Grove, IL: IVP Academic, 2011. Explores the movement from seniors to elders along with significant medical perspective on dementia.

*Johnson, Richard. *Caring for Aging Parents: Straight Answers That Help You Serve Their Needs without Ignoring Your Own*. St. Louis, MO: Concordia Publishing House, 1995.

————. *Creating a Successful Retirement*. Liguori, MO: Liguori, 1999.

————. *Parish Ministry for Maturing Adults: Principles, Plans and Bold Proposals*. New London, CT: Twenty-Third Publications, 2007.

Koenig, Harold G. *Aging and God: Spiritual Pathways to Mental Health in Midlife and Later Years*. New York: Haworth Pastoral Press, 1994.

*Kruschwitz, Robert, ed. *Aging: Christian Reflection*. Waco, TX: The Center for Christian Ethics at Baylor University, 2003. This book offers both chapters that explore calling, spirituality, and caring for the aged and chapters that review the aging literature.

Maitland, David J. *Aging as Counterculture*. New York: Pilgrim Press, 1991. An exploration of the experience of aging as being countercultural.

Menconi, Peter. *The Intergenerational Church: Understanding Congregations from WWII to WWW.com*. Littleton, CO: Mt. Sage Publishing, 2010.

Moberg, David O. *Aging and Spirituality*. New York: Haworth Pastoral Press, 2001.

Nash, Laura, and Howard Stevenson. *Just Enough: Tools for Creating Success in Your Work and Life*. Hoboken, NJ: John Wiley and Sons, 2004. While not about aging, this book researches deeply the dimensions of what it means to live a full and successful life.

Nelson, John, and Richard Bolles. *What Color Is Your Parachute for Retirement*. Berkeley, CA: Ten Speed Press, 2010. The classic book reminted for retirement.

Neuhaus, Richard. *The Eternal Pity: Reflections on Dying*. Notre Dame: University of Notre Dame Press, 2000. A profound meditation on death.

Nouwen, Henri J. M. *Our Greatest Gift: A Meditation on Dying and Caring*. New York: HarperOne, 1994.

————. *A Spirituality of Caregiving*. Nashville, TN: Upper Room Books, 2011.

*Nouwen, Henri J. M., and Walter J. Gaffney. *Aging.* New York: Doubleday, 1974.

*Packer, James I. *Finishing Our Course with Joy.* Wheaton, IL: Crossway, 2014. A brief but rich treatment of finishing well.

Palmer, Parker J. *Let Your Life Speak: Listening for the Voice of Vocation.* San Francisco: Jossey-Bass, 2000. While not about aging, this book contains many insights on learning from one's life.

Parsley, Ross. *Messy Church: A Multigenerational Mission for God's Family.* Colorado Springs, CO: David C. Cook, 2012.

*Penfield, Wilder. *The Second Career: The Other Essays and Addresses.* Boston: Little, Brown & Co., 1963. An older book proposing a post-retirement calling.

Rohr, Richard. *Falling Upward: A Spirituality for the Two Halves of Life.* San Francisco: Jossey-Bass, 2011. A rich and dense book on the first and second periods of life.

Sell, Charles. *Transitions: The Stages of Adult Life.* Chicago: Moody, 1985.

*Small, Dwight Hervey. *When Christians Retire: Finding Your Purpose in the Bonus Years.* Kansas City, MO: Beacon Hill Press, 2000. A very fine exploration of retirement based on Scripture, Christian tradition, and the author's experience.

Smith, Gordon. *Courage and Calling: Embracing Your God-Given Potential.* Downers Grove, IL: IVP Books, 1999. As the title suggests, this book focuses on vocational discernment.

Stevens, R. Paul. "Death." In *Down-to-Earth Spirituality.* Downers Grove, IL: InterVarsity Press, 2003. A chapter on death in a book about Jacob.

———. *Work Matters: Lessons from Scripture.* Grand Rapids: Eerdmans, 2012. Exploring work from Genesis to Revelation.

Thibault, Jane M., and Richard L. Morgan. *Pilgrimage into the Last Third of Life: Seven Gateways for Spiritual Growth.* Nashville: Upper Room Books, 2012.

Thomas, Bill. *Second Wind: Navigating the Passage to a Slower, Deeper, and More Connected Life.* New York: Simon & Schuster, 2014.

*Tournier, Paul. *Learn to Grow Old.* Trans. Edwin Hudson. Louisville: Westminster John Knox Press, 1991. An understanding of aging rich in experience and spiritual insights.

———. *The Seasons of Life.* Eugene, OR: Wipf and Stock, 2012.

Trueblood, E. *The Common Ventures of Life: Marriage, Birth, Work, and Death.* New York: Harper & Row, 1949.

*Wright, Walter C. Jr., and Max De Pree. *The Third Third of Life: Preparing* *for Your Future.* Downers Grove, IL: InterVarsity Press, 2012. A study guide that has many resources woven into the exercises.

2. Theological Resources

Cullmann, Oscar. *Immortality of the Soul or Resurrection of the Dead?* London: Epworth, 1958. Explores the contrast between the Greek and biblical views of life after death.

*Hauerwas, Stanley et al., eds. *Growing Old in Christ.* Grand Rapids: Eerdmans, 2003. A rich resource by several authors especially helpful in biblical research and the writings of the early church on aging.

Lyon, K. Brynolf. *Toward a Practical Theology of Aging.* Philadelphia: Fortress Press, 1985. While somewhat dated, this book provides both biblical and theological resources for a theology of aging.

*Meilaender, Gilbert. *Should We Live Forever? The Ethical Ambiguities of Aging.* Grand Rapids: Eerdmans, 2013. A theologically deep analysis of the movement to extend life indefinitely.

*Wolff, Hans Walter. *Anthropology of the Old Testament.* Trans. Margaret Kohl. Philadelphia: Fortress Press, 1974. Magnificent biblical research on youth, aging, and stages of life.

3. Classic Resources

*Baxter, Richard. *The Saints' Everlasting Rest.* Ed. John T. Wilkinson. Vancouver: Regent College Publishing, 1962/2004.

Bunyan, John. *Pilgrim's Progress.* Ed. Roger Sharrock. Harmondsworth, UK: Penguin, 1965/1984.

Donne, John. *Devotions upon Emergent Occasions.* Ann Arbor: University of Michigan Press, 1624/1959.

*Hancock, Maxine. "Aging as a Stage of the Heroic Pilgrimage of Faith: Some Literary and Theological Lenses for 'Revisioning' Age." *Crux* 47, no. 1 (Spring 2011).

*Perkins, William. "Treatise on Calling." In I. Breward, ed., *The Courtenay Library of Reformation Classics, III: The Work of William Perkins.* Appleford, UK: The Sutton Courtenay Press, 1970.

Stannard, David E. *The Puritan Way of Death.* New York: Oxford University Press, 1977.

Taylor, Jeremy. *Holy Living and Dying: With Prayers Containing the Complete Duty of a Christian.* New York: D. Appleton, 1989.

4. Secular and Multidisciplinary Studies

Adams, Michael. *Stayin' Alive: How Canadian Baby Boomers Will Work, Play, and Find Meaning in the Second Half of Their Adult Lives.* Toronto: Penguin Group/Viking Canada, 2010.

Bibby, Reginald W. *The Boomer Factor: What Canada's Most Famous Generation Is Leaving Behind.* Toronto: Bastion Books, 2006.

Bouwer, J., ed. *Successful Ageing, Spirituality, and Meaning: Multidisciplinary Perspectives.* Leuven, Holland: Peeters, 2010. Academic articles on sociology, psychology, ethics, anthropology, and spirituality. The chapter on a practical theological perspective on ageing (by Jonkers) is excellent, finding human dignity in "beings-in-relation."

Bridges, William. *Transitions: Making Sense of Life's Changes.* 2nd ed. Boston: Da Capo Press, 2004.

Dychtwald, Ken, and Dan Kadlec. *The Power Years: A User's Guide to the Rest of Your Life.* Hoboken, NJ: Wiley, 2005.

Freedman, Marc. *Encore: Finding Work That Matters in the Second Half of Life.* New York: Perseus Books, 2007.

Gurian, Michael. *The Wonder of Aging: A New Approach to Embracing Life after Fifty.* New York: Atria Books/Simon & Schuster, 2013.

Jacobs, Ruth Harris. "Becoming Sixty." In Sandra Martz, ed., *When I Am an Old Woman.* Watsonville, CA.: Papier-Mache Press, 1991.

Kelcourse, Felicity, ed. *Human Development and Faith: Life-Cycle Stages of Body, Mind, and Soul.* Atlanta: Chalice Press, 2004.

Kimble, M. A. et al., eds. *Aging, Spirituality, and Religion.* Minneapolis: Augsburg Fortress, 1995. A massive, multi-authored book with many articles covering pastoral care of the aging, congregational ministry, and community outreach, with a multifaceted section on theological perspectives. Based on a multidisciplinary conference funded by the Lilly Endowment.

Koenig, Harold G. *Aging and God: Spiritual Pathways to Mental Health in Midlife and Later Years.* London: Routledge, 1994.

Orr, Robert D. *Medical Ethics and the Faith Factor: A Handbook for Clergy and Health Care Professionals.* Grand Rapids: Eerdmans, 2009.

Thomas, William H. *What Are Old People For? How Elders Will Save the World.* Acton, MA: Vander Wyk and Burnham, 2004.

*Vaillant, George. *Aging Well.* New York: Little, Brown, 2002. A very significant longitudinal study drawing valuable conclusions about successful aging. A basic text.

*Young, Michael, and Tom Schuller. *Life after Work: The Arrival of the Ageless Society.* London: HarperCollins, 1991. A British treatment on the subject of work and aging.

Zelinski, Ernie J. *The Joy of Not Working: A Book for the Retired, Unemployed, and Overworked.* Berkeley, CA: Ten Speed Press, 2003.

5. Other Religious Approaches

*Chittister, Joan. *The Gift of Years: Growing Older Gracefully.* Katonah, NY: BlueBridge, 2008. Takes a theistic approach and explores many themes of aging.

Richmond, Lewis. *Aging as a Spiritual Practice: A Contemplative Guide to Growing Older and Wiser.* New York: Gotham Books, 2012.Takes a Buddhist approach.

*Schachter-Shalomi, Zalman, and Ronald S. Miller. *From Age-ing to Sage-ing: A Revolutionary Approach to Growing Older.* New York: Grand Central Publishing, 1995. Takes a Jewish approach.

6. Theology of Disability Approaches

Brock, Brian, and John Swinton. *Disability in the Christian Tradition: A Reader.* Grand Rapids: Eerdmans, 2012.

Dawn, Marva J. *Being Well When We Are Ill: Wholeness and Hope in Spite of Infirmity.* Minneapolis: Fortress Press, 2008.

Reinders, Hans S. *Receiving the Gift of Friendship: Profound Disability, Theological Anthropology, and Ethics.* Grand Rapids: Eerdmans, 2008.

Reynolds, Thomas E. *Vulnerable Communion: A Theology of Disability and Hospitality.* Grand Rapids: Baker, 2008.

Yong, Amos. *The Bible, Disability, and the Church: A New Vision of the People of God.* Grand Rapids: Eerdmans, 2011.

Index

Abraham, 52-54
Accountability groups, 153
Adam and Eve, 160, 162, 165
Age-retardation, 162
Aging: cultural views on, 46-47;
    in New Testament, 48-50, 58-
    59; in Old Testament, 47-48,
    50-59; in Psalms, 50-52; in
    wisdom books, 50-52. *See also*
    Calling; Spiritual journey;
    Vices; Virtues
Alms deeds, 108-9; corporal
    alms deeds, 108; spiritual alms
    deeds, 108-9
Anger, 89-90
Anna, 49
Aquinas, Thomas, 108-9
Asceticism, 76-78
Auden, W. H., 79
Augustine: calling of, 40-41; on
    communion with God, 32; on
    envy, 88; on loss of friends, 147;
    on lust, 95; on rest in God, 172;
    on the resurrection of the body,
    169

Avarice, 91-92

Babbage, Stuart, 107
Banks, Julie, 77
Banks, Robert, 77
Baxter, Richard, 90, 173-75
Being *vs.* doing, 73-75
Benedict, Saint, 47-48, 87
Bianchi, Eugene: on attitudes
    toward retirement, 16-17; on
    contemplation in second half
    of life, 75; on dealing with
    challenges of aging, 73; on the
    history of reflecting on death,
    151; on midlife transition, 70;
    on numbering one's days, 51; on
    stagnation, 143; on the univer-
    salization of love, 112
Bolles, Richard, 144
Bonhoeffer, Dietrich, 24
Boulter, Stan, 144-45
Bucket lists, 78
Buechner, Frederick, 151-52

Calling: *vs.* career, 16, 31-32;